Horror Films

R. H. W. Dillard

MONARCH PRESS

Standard Book Number: 671-08104-7

Library of Congress Catalog Card Number: 75-23546

Designed by Denise Biller

Published by
MONARCH PRESS
a division of Simon & Schuster, Inc.
1 West 39th Street
New York, N.Y. 10018

For Fred & Susan Chappell

That rather than injustices and generals,
We choose to live with vampires, demons, ghouls.

CONTENTS

AUTHOR

R. H. W. DILLARD is Professor of English and Director of the
Creative Writing Program at Hollins College, Virginia. In addition
to writing numerous stories and essays, he is the author of three
volumes of poetry and a novel, *The Book of Changes*. He is the
co-author of the movie *Frankenstein Meets the Space Monster*.

ACKNOWLEDGMENTS

The photographs in this book are courtesy of the following: *The Film Journal*, John Baxter, Cinemabilia, the Film Stills Archive of the Museum of Modern Art, Bryanston Pictures, United Artists, Universal, and Warner Brothers.

PREFACE

In 1966 when I set out to write an essay on the horror film as a meaningful art form for W. R. Robinson's book, *Man and the Movies*, I felt compelled to take an evangelical tone, a crying out in the wilderness designed to batter down sturdy walls of prejudice with the sheer force of utterance and belief. Today such a performance is as unnecessary as it seemed necessary then. A number of books of film history and criticism about the genre have appeared during the decade following the appearance of my essay, among them these especially important ones: Carlos Clarens' *An Illustrated History of the Horror Film* (1967), Ivan Butler's *The Horror Film* (1967, revised in 1970 as *Horror in the Cinema*), Denis Gifford's *Karloff, The Man, The Monster, The Movies* (1973), Joel E. Siegel's *Val Lewton: The Reality of Terror* (1973), David Pirie's *A Heritage of Horror: The English Gothic Cinema 1946-1972* (1973), Arthur Lennig's *The Count: The Life and Films of Bela "Dracula" Lugosi* (1974), Paul M. Jensen's *Boris Karloff and His Films* (1974), and Calvin Thomas Beck's *Heroes of the Horrors* (1975). Even Andrew Sarris has admitted Tod Browning, Robert Siodmak, Jacques Tourneur, Edgar G. Ulmer, and James Whale to at least tenuous positions in his catalogue of American directors worthy of serious attention, *The American Cinema: Directors and Directions 1929-1968*. And Whale and Browning, along with Murnau and Dreyer, Ulmer and Freund, are beginning to receive serious attention in the film journals, while directors of the stature of Bergman and Fellini, Orson Welles, Roman Polanski, Ken Russell and Nicolas Roeg have either alluded directly in their films to their debts to the American horror film or have extended their work directly into the genre.

What all of this newfound respectability does is to free those of us who are interested in the horror film from the necessity of evangelism and its attendant overstatements and polemical positions and to give us the opportunity to examine horror films as esthetic entities, to assess their integrity, to determine their values and to apply what they offer us to the enhancement of our direct experience. In other words, we may treat them as works of art without apology or argument.

I have attempted in this book, by a close analysis of four horror films, to examine just how the horror film is a valid and meaningful artistic genre directly related to our direct experience. I should like here to acknowledge the help of a number of people without whose enthusiasm, encouragement, and assistance I could not have done the job. First of all, W. R. Robinson and George Garrett both roused me to translate my interest in horror films into useful action, and they gave me the chance in *Man and the Movies* to be heard. And Robinson gave me an approach to understanding film as a narrative art which has never let me down. Thomas R. Atkins, editor of *The Film Journal*, and Paula Putney, editor of *Contempora*, gave me the chance to develop my thinking for this book in their magazines in which the bulk of it has appeared in somewhat different form. Sarah Trott, Michael Mayo, Deborah Brumfield and Carol Williams assisted me in seeing the films (far more than are mentioned in the book) and offered me their insights as well. Anna Lewis helped me to a fuller understanding of *Frankenstein* and of Whale's work in general, Fred Chappell pointed out some subtleties in *The Wolf Man* that I had missed, Frank Doak introduced me to *Night of the Living Dead* and gave me considerable insight into its making and makers, and Mary Ann Johnson, Kathy O'Keefe and Larry Roetzel all shared with me their understanding of *Satyricon*.

I should also like to thank the Ford Foundation and Hollins College for the grant and leave of absence which enabled me to do much of the work on this book.

R. H. W. Dillard

DRAWING THE CIRCLE

The genre of the horror film dates back to the beginnings of cinema as a narrative form. Georges Méliès' film fantasies gave film its genuine narrative beginnings in the last decade of the nineteenth century; the first film version of *Dr. Jekyll and Mr. Hyde* was produced in Chicago in 1908, and the first *Frankenstein* was released by Edison in 1910. From these first crude beginnings until today, the horror film has flourished as a popular and often an artistic form — in Germany during the silent era; in America, England, Italy and around the world in the sound years. Someday we shall no doubt be reading histories of the Malaysian vampire film with the same interest that we presently accord a book like David Pirie's study of the British gothic cinema.

My purpose in this book is not, however, historical or even judicially critical. Clarens and Pirie and Ivan Butler have done their jobs well, and there is no need to go over that ground again. There has occurred a general reduction in the parabolic nature of the European and American horror film which does deserve comment here, however, before I go on into my discussion of the particular values being expressed in four horror films, which are in many ways typical of the times in which they were made.

1 /

The early horror films, those made in Germany between 1913 and 1930 and the major American horror films of the 1930s, were openly metaphysical in their concerns, even when those concerns were also social and political as in the case of *The Cabinet of Dr. Caligari (Das Kabinett des Dr. Caligari)*. That film and *The Student of Prague (Student von Prag)*, *The Golem (Der Golem)* and *Nosferatu*, and the American films they influenced (which were in many cases directed by German directors), such as Tod Browning's *Dracula*, James Whale's *Frankenstein* and *Bride of Frankenstein*, Karl Freund's *The Mummy* and *Mad Love*, Edgar G. Ulmer's *The Black Cat*, and Victor Halperin's *White Zombie* — all of these films, along with Carl Dreyer's *Vampyr*, were fully committed to an exploration of essential human nature, of what it means to be an

The Cabinet of Dr. Caligari *is expressionistic and openly metaphysical in its concerns.*

*In **Dracula** the choice is between the darkness and the light.*

individual human being, free in a complex and mysterious world to choose between an understanding of that world which is creative or decreative, to choose, in other words, between the darkness or the light.

The films of the 1940s, which were mainly American, reduced the range of that parabolic quest from the spirit to the flesh, from the metaphysical to the psychological. Finding their roots in the sexual and psychological concerns of earlier films like Florey's *Murders in the Rue Morgue*, Lambert Hillyer's *Dracula's Daughter*, and Mamoulian's *Dr. Jekyll and Mr. Hyde*, the films of the 1940s defined the human being primarily as a physical (as opposed to spiritual) being. The human psyche was no longer capable of the metaphysical yearning and force of a Henry Frankenstein, but rather became the victim of mental aberration which should be

3 /

The Mummy *is an exploration of essential human nature in a complex and mysterious world.*

cured. Victor Fleming's *Dr. Jekyll and Mr. Hyde* is a Freudian and specifically sexual film, more akin to Hitchcock's *Spellbound* than to either Stevenson's novella or the early horror films. Waggner's *The Wolf Man,* although a great deal more complex than *Spellbound*, is nevertheless cast in the terms of a Freudian psychological understanding, and in Robert Siodmak's *Son of Dracula,* Kay's morbid psychology which predisposes her to vampirism is more truly the heart of the film than Count Alucard — Dracula himself. Even Frankenstein's monster is reduced to a medical problem in his film appearances from *Son of Frankenstein* to *House of Dracula*, and in the latter of those films Larry Talbot is finally cured of his lycanthropic problems by an operation on his skull. It is appropriate that Val Lewton's shadowy and psychological films, from *The Cat People* in 1942 through *The Body Snatcher* in 1945, dominate the period, for they are concerned with expressing (as Joel E. Siegel's book title suggests) "the reality of terror" rather than the larger horrors and realities of the mind and spirit which the earlier horror film managed at least to suggest.

In the 1950s and 1960s, the American horror film sunk into a terrible decline, its concerns limited to teenage psychological malaise in films like *I Was a Teenage Werewolf, I Was a Teenage Frankenstein* and their considerable progeny, or to the over-lush romance of Roger Corman's colorful renderings of Poe's stories. The period's best films were those from Britain which Pirie discusses so well in *A Heritage of Horror*, but even those films placed a powerful emphasis upon the flesh and its literal blood and guts, rather than upon any serious attempt to redefine what it is to be human in any larger sense. As Pirie points out, the English gothic tradition may be properly seen as Byronic. The American films of the 1930s were also Romantic in their sources, but were more properly Mary Shelley's than Lord Byron's (who was very significantly debunked in the satirical portrait of him in the prologue to *Bride of Frankenstein*).

The ultimate reduction of the parabolic goals of the horror film was reached in the late 1960s and early 1970s by films like George Romero's *Night of the Living Dead* and Tobe Hooper's *The Texas Chain Saw Massacre*, films which reduce human identity literally to meat, nihilistic exercises in the expression of human

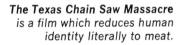

The Texas Chain Saw Massacre
is a film which reduces human identity literally to meat.

Blood for Dracula *finds parody to be the most effective approach to the traditional horror film.*

failure and insignificance. Hooper's film in particular is more akin to EC horror comics and British films like Arthur Crabtree's *Horrors of the Black Museum* and Freddie Francis's *Tales From the Crypt* than the films of either the 1930s or 1940s. It is small wonder, in the light of these films, that Paul Morrisey's *Andy Warhol's Frankenstein* and *Blood for Dracula* and Mel Brook's *Young Frankenstein* found parody to be the most effective approach to the traditional horror film. In Romero and Hooper's world, laughter may be the only salvation.

If this account of the devolution of values in the horror film is accurate, as I believe it to be, then a book on the usefulness of the horror film as an esthetic aid to the extension of individual moral consciousness would seem to be an exercise in futility. The answer to this dilemma, to my mind, lies in the horror film's vital movement into the work of major "mainstream" filmmakers, in the works of directors like Dreyer (especially in *Vampyr* and *Day of Wrath* [*Vredens Dag*]), Luis Buñuel, Georges Franju (*Eyes Without* a Face [*Les Yeux sans Visage*]), Hitchcock (especially in *The Birds*), Federico Fellini (in the "Toby Dammit" sequence of *Spirits of the Dead* and *Satyricon*), Ingmar Bergman (especially in *Hour of the Wolf* [*Vargtimmen*]), Orson Welles (from the specific allusions to horror films in *Citizen Kane* on), and younger directors like Roman Polanski (particularly in his work since *Repulsion*), Peter Bogdanovich (in *Targets* and even to some degree in the gothic grimness of *The Last Picture Show*), Ken Russell (especially in *The Devils*), Nicolas Roeg (in *Performance*, which he directed with Donald Cammell, and in *Don't Look Now*), and Brian De Palma (in *Sisters* and *Phantom of the Paradise*). The films of these directors (and others like them who have absorbed the horror tradition into their own work) are the real horror films of today, and, with rare exception, not those triple-feature bloodbaths at the local drive-in. And their interests and concerns are, for the most part, those of serious artists pressing their art to the service of the individual moral consciousness.

Any useful discussion of the possible application of the serious horror film to the enhancement of direct experience requires some understanding of what it is that the individual moral consciousness

The Devils *is one of the real horror films of today.*

requires of a work of art. If we can accept the contemporary perception of man as an active being, then an experiential art must be active and moving itself. "Mind," according to John Dewey in *Art as Experience*, "is primarily a verb," and art must celebrate "with peculiar intensity the moments in which the past reenforces the present and in which the future is a quickening of what is now." Such an art must express "the readiness of objects to move," and ultimately it must free us from "The conception that objects have fixed and unalterable values." "It is only in great art," Joyce Cary insists in *Art and Reality*, "that we move freely in a world which is at once concept and feeling, rational order and common emotion, in a dream which is truer than actual life and a reality which is only there made actual, complete and purposeful to our experience." What they are both emphasizing is the necessity for free moral movement in a world of change and the necessity for an art which realizes that possibility in its formal ordering of free motion into esthetic fact — in other words, an art, not of absolutes, but of possibilities.

Such an art would appear to be the only valid esthetic response to our present biological and cosmological understanding. "I live on earth at present," says Buckminster Fuller in *I Seem to Be a Verb*, "and I don't know what I am. I know that I am not a category. I am not a thing — a noun. I seem to be a verb, an evolutionary process — an integral function of the universe." As a verb, the individual has as his very nature the necessity to act, to join consciously the process of evolution and the universe. Emerson defined human life as "an apprenticeship to the truth that around every circle another can be drawn," and Fuller echoes that definition and enlarges it: "Whenever I draw a circle, I immediately want to step out of it. I always start with the universe: An organization of regenerative principles frequently manifest as energy systems of which all our experiences, and possible experiences, are only local instances."

In evolution, things grow toward a greater variety and complexity of form. That growth is at the center of human life as well. The human consciousness demands growth if it is to remain vital and morally sound. "The will," as Colin Wilson says in *The Occult*, "feeds on enormous vistas; deprived of them, it collapses." An art which is moral by being "actual, complete and purposeful to our experience" must, then, be an art of free motion, offering to the individual consciousness the possibility of growth in a context of universal growth.

The medium of film is one of moving light, shadow and sound, of the direct play of energy. It demands of an artist (and of a viewer) that he see experience in those terms. The artist shapes that medium to his own sense of rhythm and form, and he must be sensitive to those qualities of his medium and to what they can teach him about his narrative matter as he is to his own direct experiential perception of that matter. Because the cinematic medium is one of moving light, shadow and sound, it offers to a sensitive artist and a viewer willing to see what is there a greater opportunity to experience the actuality of existential and evolutionary possibility in meaningful forms than possibly any other artistic medium.

It is fair and even necessary to demand of a film that it be both true to life and to its medium, no matter how fanciful or unreal its texture and substance may seem. Any judgment of the real value of horror films must, then, depend upon what they offer the viewer — how they enlarge or diminish his sense of himself and of his own value, how they are true to life in its largest sense, and how they are true to the medium of film.

What I wish to do in this book is to examine four films as esthetic entities in an attempt to arrive at some sense of what the films are, of how they use the elements of the medium for the creation of value, of what precisely are the limits of the circles they draw: *Frankenstein* (1931), to my mind, along with Dryer's *Vampyr*, the finest of the films of the 1930s and one of the most fully realized of all films in the genre; *The Wolf Man* (1941), an interesting and valuable film, one of the best of the 1940s, which has received almost no serious critical attention; *Night of the Living Dead* (1968), the most successful of the nihilistic new horror films, which has gained an extraordinary underground cinematic reputation and an equally extraordinary financial success; and Fellini's *Satyricon* (1969), the fullest, richest horror film yet made.

FRANKENSTEIN:
"WHAT CHANGES DARKNESS INTO LIGHT?"

Frankenstein is, according to the horror-film historian Carlos Clarens, "the most famous horror movie of all time," and, as John Baxter says in *Hollywood in the Thirties,* "deservedly so." Frances Marion in her autobiographical *Off With Their Heads!* recalls the "curious fact" that even in Hollywood "scarcely anyone old or young in the audience viewed the picture without some nerve-tingling reaction" when it was first shown in 1931. And the film still retains most of its impact, despite the familiarity of the monster's features even to those who are seeing it for the first time. Ivan Butler reports that the "first sight of Karloff . . . still manages to shock," and it has been my experience with recent showings of the film that it can still hold its own with an initially uninterested or even hostile audience — which cannot be said for Tod Browning's *Dracula,* Karl Freund's *The Mummy* or Victor Halperin's *White Zombie.*

The source of *Frankenstein*'s continuing popular strength does not really lie in its shock value, for audiences don't scream at it the way they used to do, or the way they still do at *Night of the Living Dead* or *The Texas Chain Saw Massacre.* It appears to lie rather in the slow transformation of that initial shock and horror into a sympathy, both for Henry Frankenstein, whose dreams have gone fatally awry, and for the monster himself. Ivan Butler has noted the depth of this sympathy and described it as "more than sympathy — a tragic sense of human potentiality wasted, destroyed by a lack of understanding which leads so quickly to panic and disaster." He attributes that sympathy to Boris Karloff's skill as an actor and to James Whale's "dignity of treatment; a respect, not only for the 'normal' people, not only for the monster, but for the whole inherent significance of his subject." When he continues by ascribing to the film "a largeness of purpose, a hint of the grandeur of mysteries beyond our knowledge," he has certainly touched the source of the film's success, and he offers a starting point for an examination of *Frankenstein's* nature.

*In **Frankenstein**, Boris Karloff's makeup is a remarkably subtle fusion of the grotesque and horrific with the recognizably human.*

However, to attempt to explain the film's largeness by examining its technical virtues is really a futile exercise. For example, most of the film's horrific quality is usually ascribed to Jack Pierce's makeup, and certainly that is true, and to Karloff's gaining sympathy for the monster despite the makeup. But an examination of photographs of earlier versions of the monster reveals that the makeup was toned down, was made more human — in an earlier version, the monster's forehead was marred by two metal rings with ropes of flesh twisted through them. For all of Karloff's genius as an actor, some of his later success must, then, be ascribed to Pierce's makeup and its remarkably subtle fusion of the grotesque and horrific with the recognizably human. And to say that the film's sense of dignity is solely the work of Whale is to deny the soundness of the screenplay by Garrett Fort and Francis Edward Faragoh or the suggestions of the first director on the picture, Robert Florey. Whale's direction is impeccable, but it is not stamped with Whale's identity to anything like the degree that his later films *The Old Dark House, The Invisible Man* or *Bride of Frankenstein* are. And certainly Arthur Edeson's photography, Clarence Kolster's editing and the sets themselves deserve proper credit, to say nothing of the acting of Colin Clive, Dwight Frye and Frederick Kerr.

The only effective approach to the film is to disregard the efforts of its makers and look directly at the thing they made, the film as an esthetic entity with its own life and qualities and values. The film is problematic as any genuine work of art must be, but it is its own solution. It has an integrity and wholeness which offers itself up, not only to emotion or even to imagination, but to understanding.

The initial problem which confronts the understanding of any horror film is that one which is involved in the approach to any work of fantasy or fable. The theme appears too readily available; a simple allegorical reading seems to milk the work of its substance all too quickly. And certainly such is the case with most horror films — an evil invades the lives of a group of people, and they repel or destroy it by their resourcefulness, their caring for each other and their faith in the general rightness of the nature of the world. A viewer may expand that allegorical reading as far as he likes, but the film itself has little more to offer. He may see a film like Robert Siodmak's *Son of Dracula* more than once, but only for the pleasure of re-covering familiar narrative ground or perhaps for the imaginative *frisson* which may be gained from, say, the image of Count Alucard floating across the dark swamp water, standing on his coffin. The film will offer his understanding very little more than it did on a first viewing. Its matter is drained by a simple rational and allegorical reading of its symbols and events; it remains as essentially abstract experience with minimal existential concretion, an experience which does not bear thorough and continuing acquaintance.

The temptation is to read *Frankenstein* in that way, allegorically and quickly. It is a temptation compounded by the Edward van Sloan introductory remarks, in which he says that it is "the story of Frankenstein, a man of science, who sought to create a man after his own image without reckoning upon God," or by Mary Shelley's explication of the film in the opening scene of *Bride of Frankenstein* when she describes it as an account of "the punishment that may befall a mortal man who dares to emulate God." That is a tidy explanation, one that would reduce the film to a retelling of the medieval Faust legend as if Goethe or the passage of several centuries had not occurred. And since James Whale did direct both pictures, that must have been what he had in mind, or so the argument goes. But van Sloan's preface is scarcely appropriate to the film and its values, and *Bride of Frankenstein*, for all its virtues, is not *Frankenstein*, and the temptation to identify them must be avoided in order to arrive at the genuine substance of *Frankenstein*.

Frankenstein does have to do with a man's overreaching himself, but the failure lies not so much in the daring or in the act, but in his inability to cope with the product of his actions. The real Mary Shelley puts it much better than her later film avatar when she has her monster point out to his creator that he has not fulfilled the duties of a creator: "Remember that I am thy creature; I ought to be thy Adam, but I am rather the fallen angel, whom

/ 14

thou drivest from joy for no misdeed." The film has much to show us about the nature of creation and its moral consequences, but even an examination of that thematic element will not exhaust the film, for it has as much to show us about the fact of death and the resiliency and strength of life in its face, about the very nature of human experience and of life itself. Frankenstein's experience and his moral pilgrimage can only be fully understood in the context of the larger texture and motion of the film itself; the form gives the matter of the film its value and meaning, just as that matter fills out and gives substance to the abstract idea of the form. The film's complex texture of physical and mental fact not only explains its thematic specifics but is actually its "meaning."

The symbols in the film are not static, nor are they exterior to the texture of the film itself. Fire, for example, carries its traditional meanings in the film, but it never appears except when it is a functional element in the narrative. It is not imposed on the film; the film creates and recreates its own symbolic levels as it goes. This narrative activity of the film's symbols is one of the major reasons why it is in this respect superior even to so fine a film as Carl Dreyer's *Vampyr*. *Vampyr* is a book film; its symbols are drawn directly from a European literary heritage (a book even serves as one of those symbols in the film). The static shots of weathervanes and still water are striking, but they are essentially extraneous to the remarkably poetic moving texture of the film itself. Only the reversal of traditional black-white symbology which reaches its functional climax with the doctor's death in the white

Dr. Jekyll and Mr. Hyde is marred by the interposition of static and exterior symbols such as the statuette of Cupid and Psyche.

flour of the mill develops into a fully cinematic and organic use of symbol in the film. Even so fluid a film as Rouben Mamoulian's *Dr. Jekyll and Mr. Hyde*, with its brilliant and completely integral metamorphosis scenes in which physical motion and moral change are identified as fully as they ever have been in any work of art, is nevertheless marred by the interposition of static and exterior symbols such as the statuette of Cupid and Psyche offering ironic commentary on Hyde's murder of Ivy.

Frankenstein is an interpretation of Mary Shelley's novel, but it is no book film. It is a thoroughly cinematic film, drawing its symbolic texture and meaning out of its own narrative movement. That the monster's life begins in lightning and ends in fire, for example, is a simple enough observation and a rewarding one, but it would be a misleading one if the whole complex pattern of fire, light and darkness were not also taken into consideration.

Frankenstein opens in darkness in a graveyard. The first shot is of a gravedigger's hands pulling up the rope with which he has lowered a coffin into a grave. The grave is seen in the context of the graveyard with its leaning crosses and an effigy of skeletal Death (who at first seems almost to be one of the graveside mourners), but those are not the vital and ongoing symbols in the scene. Rather the fact of death and the literal darkness become symbolic when the gravedigger strikes a match to light his pipe, introducing fire in the film to darkness and death. By the light of

*In **Frankenstein** the fact of darkness and literal death become symbolic when the gravedigger strikes a match to light his pipe.*

the moon, a dim and reflected natural light partially obscured by night clouds, Henry Frankenstein and Fritz set about robbing the grave and then cutting down a hanging corpse from a gallows. During these activities, Fritz carries a lantern. His clothes are also much darker than those of Frankenstein, and Fritz is thus texturally more closely involved with fire, darkness and death than is Frankenstein. This initial context establishes a pattern which develops throughout the rest of the picture. Elizabeth, Victor and Doctor Waldman are introduced by lamplight, fire tamed to civilized uses, and their symbolic context in the film is one of ordinary light rather than darkness and fire. When Henry reveals that he has been searching for a ray beyond the ultraviolet, "the great ray that first brought light into the world," his ambiguous relation to fire and darkness is explained; he moves through a context of fire and darkness seeking a light beyond seeing, the answer to the very question, "What changes darkness into light?" The movement of the first part of the film is that of Henry's search through darkness for the source of light and life, against the advice of Doctor Waldman, Elizabeth and Victor, none of whom can really see into that darkness because of their civilized vision of tamed light, with the assistance of the hunchbacked Fritz who is integrally a part of that darkness. In this part of the film, only Henry is a free agent, moving purposefully through a dark context; it is Henry who literally flings dirt in Death's face in the cemetery. Fritz merely does his bidding, unencumbered by either higher vision or normal daylight vision, and Doctor Waldman, Elizabeth and Victor merely react to Henry's actions which they cannot properly see or understand.

Henry literally flings dirt in **Death's face in the cemetery.**

The actual creation scene is literally an explosion of the higher light into the darkness, guided by Henry Frankenstein (in white clothes) with the aid of Fritz (dressed in black). The shrill electricality of the scene is certainly appropriate to its content. Light and dark tangle and crackle in the atmosphere and dance wildly down into the laboratory. The monster's inert form with its skin noticeably dark and dead is raised into the night to the light — the lightning, that most active and meaningful fusion of light and fire. When it is lowered back into the room, the rigid dark hand has now relaxed. And when that hand moves with a wondrous grace, Henry cries out, "It's moving! It's alive!" At that moment, he has achieved a triumph that enlarges the scale by which humanity must be measured. He has joined the light and the dark (and, despite his lack of awareness, the fire) into an electrical tension which is life itself. He has repeated in small the original creation of man by joining earth and air (flesh and spirit) together — a joining made symbolically specific by the infusion of the lightning's life into a body pieced together from dead bodies dug up from the earth. He has become what Mary Shelley wished him to be, "The Modern Prometheus."

Henry Frankenstein is, then, in the first part of the film an heroic figure, the moral free agent who can see that the apparently fixed distinctions between light and darkness, life and death are not unalterable. And he acts upon his vision. But his triumph is, like his creation, inextricably involved with his defeat. The end *is* in the beginning. After the harnessing of the great ray and its gift of movement and life to his creature, Henry relaxes under a bright light, dressed in light clothes, speaking lyrically of doing the dangerous and pressing beyond. When Doctor Waldman warns him that "You have created a monster, and it will destroy you," Henry replies calmly, "Wait until I bring him into the light." Even the revelation that the monster's brain is a criminal brain gives him only a moment's pause. But he is smoking a cigar, and fire is present in the relaxed scene, however tamed and harmless. When he hears of the brain, he abruptly removes the cigar and puts it down. Then the monster makes his first full appearance, and light, darkness and fire, earth and air, come actively together, not to be successfully parted until the final scene of the film.

Henry darkens the room. The monster backs through the door and then turns to face his creator, moving from shadows into a lighter context. Frankenstein shows no revulsion or dismay towards what he has created — the first irrefutable proof of his blindness to certain essential values of the light, for his creature is huge and ugly, an emblem of death in life. As Ivan Butler puts it, "His gaunt features and dark-socketed eyes have a true charnel-house appearance." But when the monster is shown sunlight for the first time, spilling down onto him from a skylight, his appealing innocence, his yearning for the light and his confused hurt when it is withdrawn reveal to the viewer the beauty that Frankenstein alone has been able to see in this monstrous figure. The monster, sewn together from dead bodies and with a criminal brain, does nevertheless yearn for air and the light like a flower. The life that animates him is the life we all share, created though he was by a fellow man. Paul Jensen reads this scene as "a small-scale allegory of man's efforts to grasp the intangible unknown, and of his bewilderment at a creator who keeps him from it." But then Fritz runs into the room with a torch, and the monster's innocent struggle to regain the lost light turns into something much uglier as darkness, earth and fire assert their ascendancy in his nature. As John Baxter points out in *Sixty Years of Hollywood*, the light for which he yearns is "a symbol of reason and grace from which he is forever barred." And, as he might have added, the monster himself is an emblem of fallen and unredeemed man. After he is subdued, he is chained in the cellar below earth level like a wild beast, tormented by Fritz with a whip and with the fire of his torch. Frankenstein turns away from his creation, betraying its potential, and he reveals his dangerous flaw.

Henry, in his idealism, has become a half man. By yearning for the light beyond seeing, he has forgotten that he is a mortal man, susceptible to error and to sin. While venturing out into the dark, he has forgotten the darkness in himself; while reaching into the air, he has forgotten the earthiness of his nature. He and Fritz have become two halves of one man — not allegorically but actually. Henry has become all brain and nerve, idealistic, daring, able to think and to do the impossible, and he uses Fritz as his body — fearful, ignorant, crippled, dark Fritz, whom Henry called "fool" in his first line in the film. They have become like Aylmer and Aminadab in Hawthorne's "The Birthmark," and Henry, like Aylmer, is striving to be more than man while forgetting what it is to be a man. In the film, Henry's forgetting is more than symbolic or even psychological; it is experientially active. He has not only forgotten his own lower self, he has also ceased to think of Fritz as a separate entity.

When Henry is forced to allow Doctor Waldman, Elizabeth and Victor to observe the act of creation, he scorns their imputation that he has gone mad. He says to them, "One man crazy, and three very sane spectators." And, of course, there are five people in the room. He has forgotten to include Fritz. In strictly narrative terms, he has forgotten the man who will teach the monster fear and hatred, who will introduce him to fire and pain, who will transform him from an innocent seeker of the light into a murderer. Fritz, whose fear and trembling give the monster his crim-

"One man crazy and three very sane spectators."

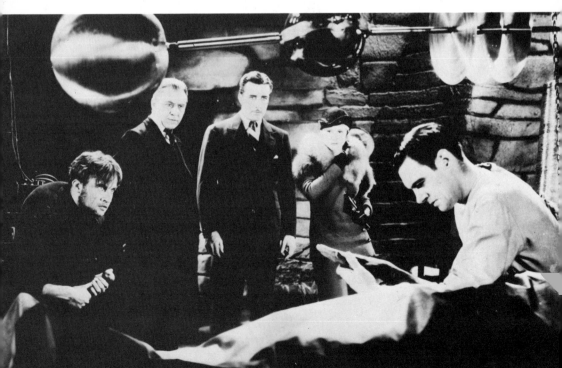

inal brain, is the agency by which the new Adam will be transformed into the new Cain. And in the symbolic terms flowing out of the narrative, Henry has forgotten what it is to be human and to be limited and, therefore, who and what he is. The future should be a quickening of what now is, but Henry's imagined future grows out of a false present, and cannot then be what he dreamed. Henry as a creator and an artist has forgotten that the imagination feeds upon the real and paradoxically causes the real to fulfill itself by that feeding. He has forgotten that his new creation is composed of dead flesh. "That body is not dead," he brags to Waldman, "It has never lived." The statement is true in the sense that any work of art or any earthly creation is something new. But, as Poe reminds us, that same work of art is the product of "multiform combinations among the things and thoughts of Time." It is this latter truth which Henry earlier expressed when he spoke of the freshly exhumed corpse in the first scene as "just resting, waiting for a new life to come," and that he has now forgotten. Henry's imagination has come to feed only upon dreams, and when the real reasserts its primacy, he cannot face what he sees. "Oh, come away, Fritz," he says, aware again of who he is and who Fritz is, "Leave it alone." But in his shocked recovery of his own identity, he blinds himself to the nature of his creation — the "him" has become again an "it" — and he betrays even the potential life his imagined future might have in a real world.

When Frankenstein loses sight of his creation's reality, he also loses his moral force and his control over Fritz. He allows Fritz to torment the monster, and when the monster turns on Fritz and kills him, Henry loses heart completely. He is able to recognize his moral responsibility for what has happened as he says of the monster (granting him again the dignity of a personal pronoun), "He hated Fritz. Fritz always tormented him," and later when he mumbles, "Oh, poor Fritz! Oh, my poor Fritz! All my fault!" But this recognition does not give him renewed vitality. He collapses, surrenders his belief in his work and passes his responsibility on to Doctor Waldman, beginning thereby a new cycle of death and darkness and forcing the dark of his creation to escape into the very light of day. He allows himself to be taken home by his father, back to a childhood dependence on a man who, by Henry's own confession, "never believes in anyone."

The Baron Frankenstein, an irascible, comic figure, represents the whole world Henry has been struggling to transcend, a world in which men are creatures of material comfort — tamed light and tamed fire — with fixed positions in an unchanging social order, a world of unalterable facts and unalterable values. The Baron cannot imagine what Henry could be doing in his laboratory, for what more could he want than a home, food and a beautiful girl? He is a kindly but utterly condescending local ruler. The good wine, he tells us, would be wasted on the servants, and the full extent of his knowledge of human nature would seem to reside in his observation that the villagers are happy on Henry's wedding day as they are drinking beer, but that tomorrow they will be fighting. He is by his own lights a good man, but his is a mundane and static goodness, stifling the possibility of genuine moral growth. His sole wish is for Henry to settle down and produce an heir — "A son to the House of Frankenstein!" — which will assure the preservation of his orderly world. The wine with which he toasts Henry's wedding was his grandmother's, as are the carefully preserved orange blossoms which have served for the weddings of the Frankensteins for decades.

It is at his father's house that we see Henry and Elizabeth for the first time in bright sunlight, sitting in comfortable ease on a terrace. Henry tells Elizabeth, "It's like heaven being with you again," and she replies, "Heaven wasn't so far away all the time, you know." The scene is the most brightly lit and romantic one in the film with one exception — the parallel scene between the monster and little Maria, a scene that proves that even in heavenly surroundings, hell is never very far away. Henry is smoking on the terrace, so that fire is present even in that romantic context, its smoke literally dividing Henry and Elizabeth while he promises not to think of "those horrible days and nights" any more, the time when he "couldn't think of anything else." And, of course, the idyllic quality of the scene has already been undercut by the preceding scene in which the monster and the darkness have entered the open air.

Frankenstein's monster, introduced so suddenly to life and light, to fire and death, gains strength as rapidly. Doctor Waldman reports in his journal as he prepares to vivisect him that he requires increasingly stronger injections to remain inert. Waldman, also a good man and the father of Henry's intellect, cannot cope with the living force that Henry has created, and shortly after sunset (after 7:30 in the evening) he prepares to kill the monster but is killed himself. The gracefully beautiful first movement of the monster's hand in the creation scene is repeated in this scene, but it has now become an expression of menace and strength. The monster raises his hand and strangles Doctor Waldman. He then stumbles clumsily downstairs in the tower, rejects the cellar of pain and death, and wanders out into the night.

The monster continues to grow in strength and skill as the film proceeds. He opens the door of the tower only accidentally, but by the time he arrives at Frankenstein's home, he is able to move silently and to open a French window. His growth into life

The two children, both left alone by their fathers, play together by the lake.

Fire even enters its natural antagonist, water.

is, however, always ironically a movement toward death — the deaths of others at his hands and finally his own. Without the guidance of his creator, he is forced to be only a creature of his senses. He leaves the tower mainly to escape the awful cellar room below the ground. He meets the little girl Maria in the sunlight by a lake, and her kindness and innocence rouse the yearning for light in him again. The two children, both left alone by their fathers, play together, tossing flowers into the lake to watch them float. But the monster cannot differentiate between Maria and a flower, so he drowns her while only hoping to see her float. Light, air and water have become as deadly for the monster as darkness, earth and fire. These elements continue to mingle dangerously for the rest of his life. After the discovery of Maria's death and the monster's attack on Elizabeth, he is tracked down by the villagers bearing torches. Fire offers the only illumination under a blurred and cloudy sky of dimly mingled light and dark, and in one striking and significant shot, fire even enters its natural antagonist, water, as the villagers' torches are shown burning in the night air and reflected beneath them in the lake. The hitherto controlled camera moves freely from high to low, moving over the water and into the barren hills as it tracks the villagers and their prey through the dark and elemental landscape.

Henry Frankenstein reassumes the moral responsibility for his creation after the attack on Elizabeth. He first attempts to protect her by locking her in her room, just as he had earlier locked his visitors in the tower and then locked his monster away. But he realizes that a man cannot simply lock up his values and his life and expect them to be safe from the dangers of day and night. He rejects the Baron's world and its preserved flowers once again when he sees the necessity to face his creation directly and handle it with his own hands (not Fritz's or Doctor Waldman's). He thinks of Elizabeth, as he had not done in his laboratory, when he places her in Victor's care — a selfless act, for Victor loves her. (Earlier Elizabeth had said lightly to Victor, "I'm far too fond of you," and

As Henry and the monster struggle, Henry rolls on the ground into the fire.

Victor had replied, "I wish you were.") His home responsibilities in relative order, Henry ventures out, dressed in a light suit, to face his dark creation. But now too late, the damage of his earlier failure beyond undoing, Henry vows not to create further (nor to redeem his creation), but to destroy: "I made him with these hands and with these hands I will destroy him." Henry is acting now in full consciousness. He admits the manhood of his creature (he calls him "him"), but his moral reactions to that man are dark ones, those of justice and vengeance.

The monster meets his maker in the mountains, and Henry meets darkness, earth and fire as he meets his creature. The monster knocks Henry's torch away, and as they struggle Henry rolls on the ground into the fire. The monster then carries him to a windmill, and there the two face each other — alone but surrounded by an angry humanity, their faces given to the audience identically as they stare at each other through a turning wooden gear in the mill, two living faces in a context of motion beyond either's control, not creator and creation now, but fellow creatures, victims each to each.

The monster was born in an abandoned watch tower, given life by the fire and light of the lightning and the great ray, the light beyond seeing. He dies, trapped and in a frenzy of fear, by fire in another tower, a windmill; Paul Jensen says that "Frankenstein's laboratory was originally to have been located in the old mill, so when the monster returns there at the film's end, it is because that is the only refuge he knows," and the Baron still refers to Henry's tower as "an old ruined windmill." The elements gave him birth, and they now conspire to give his life back to the air and him to death. He hurls his creator from him like a broken doll, almost as if the life of them both were contained solely in the monster. But it is the creator who survives, saved by the vanes of the windmill and dropped back safely to the ground. Earth and fire, joined by the gravedigger in the initial scene, separate again, as Henry comes finally to earth and his creation is destroyed by fire, the only light which was ever given him without denial.

The final scene in the film takes place in the light. Henry is restored to a comforting Elizabeth, but he is a figure in the dis-

*The last real shot is a descent away from the windmill,
itself a torch now against a dark sky.*

tance, seen through a doorway. The Baron is in the foreground, talking to the maids about his grandmother's wine again. The door is closed, and the Baron repeats his toast. "Here's . . . Here's to a son to the House of Frankenstein." But it is his toast; it is not shared by Elizabeth and Henry. There may well be a son, but the order of the Baron's world has been forever shattered, for all the appearances to the contrary. The Baron gets the last word, but the last real scene in the film was at the burning windmill, the last real shot a descent away from that windmill, itself a torch now against a dark sky. It is no wonder that Orson Welles copied this shot so scrupulously at the end of *Citizen Kane*, for both films close with the burning of a great man's dream and the camera's appropriate withdrawal down and away from the ruins. The last time we see Henry's face clearly is there, by firelight, the face of a broken hero but of a man who has dared look himself and his actions directly in the face.

The texture of the film will not allow an easy triumph of the tamed light of the Baron's house. The Baron's preserved orange blossoms are no longer in evidence, but there are fresh flowers in

Henry's room by his bed. The light which finally shapes the film is the whole pattern of light and shadow and fire. We first see Henry's face in a domestic context at Elizabeth's home, where her framed picture of Henry shares the frame with a burning candle. The whole movement of the film indicates that for Henry, the man who dared to be free, the light will never be free of the flame, or of the night.

If the pattern of light and dark in the film helps enrich the moral and thematic ambiguity of the conclusion, another structural pattern certainly helps to shape that ending. The movement in the film is not primarily horizontal, but vertical — a movement which the film shares with much Romantic art. Henry Frankenstein strives to transcend his earthbound mortality; he wants to discover just one answer, "what eternity is, for example," and he dares ask that question and act to answer it. He reaches to the heavens for his answer, just as his monster reaches upward for the light and was raised to the lightning for his birth. The film is an elaborate structure of vertical movements to match and give esthetic substance to Henry's striving (and that of his creation), but for all the striving and movement upward, the general movement of the film is downward.

The clearest vertical movement in the film's structure is the plot's. From a hillside graveyard up to the tower, the narrative then moves down into the village as the monster and Henry descend to the depths of what they are. The film rises again to the windmill and those two characters' mutual recognition of themselves and of each other. But that movement is halted by fire. The monster dies in the collapsing windmill, pressed to the floor by a fallen beam, and Henry falls to the earth and is taken back down to his home. (The Burgomaster says, "Take him down to the village, and let's get him home.")

All of the upward movements in the film are concluded by a movement down. The coffin is buried and then dug up, but the body in it returns to earth in the dying monster's form. Fritz climbs the gallows, but only to cut down the corpse and leap after it himself. Frankenstein's first command to Fritz, his first words in

The monster's and Henry's mutual recognition of themselves and each other.

the film, are, "Down, down, you fool!" His commands later to Victor and then to the monster echo those first words; he tells them both to "Sit down!" All of Fritz's journeys up and down the stairs in the tower end in his death by hanging (a last small up and down) in the cellar room. Henry comes down from the tower to the village himself in defeat. And the monster's first journey as a free man is to come down the tower steps and on down into the village.

The camera moves into the village and up to the Burgomaster's door on Henry's wedding day — an upward movement that reveals the town at its most cheerily innocent and happiest. But Ludwig follows that exact journey carrying little Maria's dead body, and the music that escorted the camera on its trip is stilled by Ludwig's movement over the same way. (Even the sock that Fritz tugs up over his skinny shanks on the steps in the tower reappears in re-

Even the sock that Fritz pulls up appears in reverse on the pulled-down sock on Maria's swinging dead leg.

verse on the pulled-down sock on Maria's swinging dead leg.) And finally the men of the village retrace that journey in reverse with burning torches as they go out to hunt down the murderer.

The chase moves up into the mountains, but that movement is also a reversal of an earlier movement rather than a new positive one. Frankenstein and his monster move back up to a windmill, only this time the creature brings his creator to the heights. The death reverses the birth, and the spent Henry is finally brought down again to his ordinary life.

What goes up, in *Frankenstein*, does finally come down. The Baron does have the last word. But the gained awareness, earned by violence and pain and death, of the necessity of the descent as well as the ascent is itself perhaps the final ascent in the film. Henry will never be able to ignore the real or the fallen again, and the audience, because of the complexity and integrity of the film's textural structure, will never itself be able to ignore either the power of the yearning for the ascent and the light, nor the awesome necessity for the descent and the darkness as well. The source of the film's largeness and of its sympathy and dignity is in that gained awareness. Mary Shelley's monster claims that human sympathy is all that he requires to become a moral man: "If any being felt emotions of benevolence towards me, I should return them a hundred and a hundredfold; for that one creature's sake I would make peace with the whole kind!" No one offers *Frankenstein*'s monster that sympathy except for an innocent child, with the possible exception of Frankenstein himself for that one moment in the windmill when he faces the monster through the turning gear. And the monster does not die at peace with humankind.

The texture of the film seems to indicate that Henry has grown morally in the course of the film, perhaps not to the heights of which he dreamed at the beginning, but to heights of perception that most men (the Baron and the villagers) never reach. But the film itself demands another ascent, the development of a genuine sympathy for the monster, the figure of horror and fear, by the audience itself. Karloff said that "Whale and I both saw the character as an innocent one" and that "What astonished us was the fantastic number of ordinary people that got this general air of sympathy." Give the credit to Karloff's astonishing performance or to Whale's direction or to the film as a whole, but that sympathy is gained and the film's ultimate moral structure finds its resolution in the individuals in the audience. That sympathy is finally the film's "meaning." Its narrative and symbolic and thematic texture is the necessary medium for that meaning's creation, its flowering in actual experience.

This discussion has by no means exhausted *Frankenstein*. If it had, it would have been its own refutation. The film's conscious and expressionistic artificiality in setting and costume, its use of flowers and of dogs, its emphasis upon the ceilings of its rooms as well as the walls and floors, the camera's movement and rhythm, the sparse and extraordinarily effective use of music, the use of numerous sets of paired characters, the film's social implications (the evil's flowing down from the upper class to the ordinary villagers), the contrasts of the solid earth with the fragility and hollowness of man's structures and even with water — all of these approaches to the film will add much more to what I have suggested here. *Frankenstein* is a genuinely vital work of art in which matter and form are actively one. It expresses the human need for growth and largeness, and it also expresses the limitations which hamper that growth and give to life both its tragic possibilities and its heroic potentialities.

THE WOLF MAN:

"THE WAY YOU WALK IS THORNY . . ."

Although it was, according to Carlos Clarens, Universal's "most successful film of the season" in 1941 and, in response to its initial popularity, Lon Chaney, Jr. went on to play Lawrence Talbot in four more films, *The Wolf Man* has never received much critical attention, even from critics who do take the horror film seriously. Carlos Clarens mentions it only in passing, and Ivan Butler discusses it in a single paragraph in his chronology of horror films. He does admit that "the misty atmospheric photography, believable script and unforced dialogue, and restrained sincere playing by Lon Chaney and others could have made this a really convincing study of the oldest and most universal of superstitions — lycanthropy." But he concludes that Chaney as the wolf man is too "clearly, and often, visible," that his makeup "bears not the slightest resemblance to any wolf that ever was," and that "Had his appearances been as shadowy and mysterious as those of Lewton's panther [in *The Cat People*], this could have been a classic of its kind." I suspect Butler's view is the generally accepted one, for Clarens also mentions the werewolf as looking "at times . . . like a hirsute Cossack."

There is no denying that, despite the care of the film's making and its early popularity, it is a lesser film than *Frankenstein*. Not only have the critics ignored it, but audiences have as well. In the winter of 1969 when I ordered a print of the film for use by a student studying horror films at Hollins College, the distributor was practically ecstatic because it had been such a long time since anyone had bothered to order it. Both the critical and popular situations have changed somewhat by now; Leonard Maltin's current edition of *TV Movies* calls it "One of the finest horror films ever made," and Calvin Thomas Beck, in *Heroes of the Horrors*, allows it to be "one of a handful of horror films deserving the label 'classic.'" But the incident nevertheless stands as evidence of the film's having fallen on hard times.

Ivan Butler's explanation of *The Wolf Man*'s failure is not a very satisfactory one. Frankenstein's monster is seen clearly and often in *Frankenstein* with no loss of shadow or mystery, and although Chaney's werewolf doesn't look like a wolf, the very title of the film suggests that he wasn't meant to. (Also, Butler has forgotten or ignored the other werewolf in the film who *does* look exactly like a wolf.) There are, of course, other explanations of a similar nature that could be offered. George Waggner is not the director that Whale is; a glance at his other films of 1941 show at least that his efforts are not of consistently high quality: *Man Made Monster*, the first Lon Chaney, Jr. horror film, is an adequate thriller with some pretensions to depth, and *Horror Island* is an amusing comedy thriller which steals from any number of serials and *The Cat and the Canary* with reckless abandon. But those films were produced respectively by Jack Bernhard and Ben Pivar, and Waggner produced *The Wolf Man* himself. It is the only one of the three that can really be considered to be *his* picture. One could also fault the reluctance of Waggner to show Lawrence Talbot's transformation from man to wolf man head-on (as Jack Pierce and Stuart Walker had managed to do quite simply and successfully in *The Werewolf of London* and as Pierce and Roy William Neill were to do later with Chaney in *Frankenstein Meets the Wolf Man*), but Waggner's insistence upon emphasizing Talbot's hands and especially his feet can be shown to have serious thematic reasons. Chaney's acting is not of the quality of Karloff's, but in the carefully controlled texture of the film, it is really exactly what is required. A genuinely satisfactory answer to the question of *The Wolf Man*'s loss of strength over the past thirty years lies deeper than any of these answers have suggested, and can only be determined by a structural and textural analysis of the film of the kind that reveals something of *Frankenstein*'s esthetic success.

The Wolf Man was made from an original screenplay by Curt Siodmak and is, therefore, not an act of translation from book to film like *Frankenstein, Dr. Jekyll and Mr. Hyde* or *Vampyr*. But it is, in conscious texture and in theme, as much a book film as either of the latter two and more so than *Frankenstein*. The first shot of the film is of a set of books, and Sir John Talbot's home is filled with books. Much of the tension in the film and in Lawrence Talbot is between his active, physical nature and the static, bookish, past-

*In **The Wolf Man,** Sir John Talbot's home is filled with books.*

The gypsy Maleva represents in the film a more primitive and instinctive kind of knowledge.

ridden society of his heritage. And, like Victor Fleming's *Dr. Jekyll and Mr. Hyde* which was also released in 1941, most of its symbolic texture is Freudian and in that sense text-bookish for all the efforts of Siodmak and Waggner to make its symbols integral and narratively functional. The theme of the struggle between the present and the past, the free active life and the restrained bookish one, more than makes up for much of the externality of the film's symbolic texture, but the resolution of that vital theme may well hold the answer to the film's apparent esthetic weakness.

    The Wolf Man, like *Frankenstein* and any other parabolic work of art, seems to open itself to a strictly allegorical interpretation. The book of the opening shot is one explaining lycanthropy in disciplined and rational terms. The film's narrative would then appear to be an acting out of an unalterably ordered phenomenon, the progress, say, of an incurable disease. The gypsy Maleva, representative in the film of a more primitive and instinctive kind of knowledge, seems to support such a reading of the tale. She, too, lives in a context of unalterable fact. "Whoever is bitten by a werewolf and lives," she tells Lawrence Talbot, "becomes a werewolf himself," and three times in the film she repeats her fatalistic credo ". . . as the rain enters the soil, the river enters the sea, so tears run to a predestined end." The film is a retelling of the story of the Fall, of an innocent's entrance into the knowledge of good and evil and its destructive effects on him. One of Talbot's earliest memories is of snitching apples with his childhood friend, Paul Montford, and his sexual attraction to Gwen Conliffe causes him to attempt to lure her away from her fiancé, a gamekeeper who offers her at least something like an edenic natural life.

But an allegorical reading won't hold up throughout the film, which continues to reveal more of itself on repeated viewing than an allegory could ever do. The film is a reenactment of the Fall, but in modern existential terms. Colonel Paul Montford, who stole apples with Talbot, is the chief constable of the village. His successful coming to terms with his loss of innocence by his full identification with the fallen society in which he lives stands as an illuminating contrast to Talbot's fall and failure. Montford maintains his stability and identity by denying his moral freedom; Larry struggles to be free and endangers his very identity. There is more than one way of repeating that primordial descent into sin and death — as many ways in fact as there are cultures or even individuals — and that pluralistic understanding is at the heart of this film, rendering it much more than simply allegory and offering the film itself the opportunity to respond successfully to that understanding or to fall.

Lawrence Talbot is, again as the title suggests, at the center of the film. His initial appearance is that of the free, whole man — a healthy, happy figure, dressed in light clothes, riding in the open sunlight in an open car. When he first visits Gwen Conliffe, he pauses under a large wall sign which reads, "SANEMAN." He is a very physical figure, larger than anyone else in the film; his father, Sir John, remarks on his size to Colonel Montford, "Big boy, isn't he?" and Montford replies, "Huge." He is also American in voice and manner, having spent eighteen years in America, and he is pragmatic like an American, used to working wth tangible things in a tangible way: "I can figure out anything if you give me electric current, tubes, wires, something I can do with my hands." He is a believer in seeing and doing, and the first thing he does in his father's home is set up and adjust a large telescope in his father's book-filled observatory as if he were bringing a whole new way of seeing to this ancient Welsh village. But, for all his emphasis upon seeing and handling the real world, his American innocence causes him to be unable to see clearly in this European context. Like one of Henry James's young Americans, he can see only what his American experience has prepared him to see. When he visits an antique shop, he sees a walking stick with a silver wolf's head as its handle, but he thinks the wolf is a dog. He seems, then, in all respects to be yet another version of the American Adam, ripe for a fall into European evil and the old serpent's knowledge.

The difference between Larry Talbot and Christopher Newman or Millie Theale is that the fall is already within him, not only in the larger sense of original sin, but also as a product of his specific blood heritage. He is not an American. He is the second son of a Welsh nobleman who went to America seeking his freedom and the new world, but he has returned home because of the death of his older brother John to take up the responsibilities of the family heritage. The potentiality of his moral freedom has already been sharply diminished in the first scene. He is not driving the open car, but is merely the passenger in his father's car, being driven by his father's chauffeur. The first use he makes of the new telescope is that of a *voyeur*, for he looks, however accidentally at first, into the window of Gwen Conliffe's room in her house in the village. Even his innocent confusion about the wolf's head already bears the marks of the fall, because he has just rejected another stick with a "little dog's head" on it when he turns to the wolf's head cane. He is innocent, not as a new Adam, but only as a young man who has not yet faced the truth of what he and all of his fellow men are. He has not yet learned what Henry Frankenstein temporarily forgets — what it is to be a man with all of a man's limitations and dark failings.

When Larry Talbot begins to feel doubts about himself and what he has always believed, he turns like a good pragmatist to his own experience and to the actual world immediately around him. His own experience tells him that he is a free man in a world of open values, but the society around him tells him something completely contradictory.

First, he is told, as he was as a child, that he is not Larry Talbot, but Lawrence Talbot or Master Larry, Sir John's son and heir to the estate. He is, unlike his brother, uncomfortable in that role, but it is now his to play. His father believes that his social position makes him safe from the intrusions of a vulgar world, or, for that matter, a fallen one. "You're Lawrence Talbot! This is Talbot Castle!" he tells his son, when Larry tells him that the men hunting the wolf are actually hunting him. "Do you believe those men could come in here and take you out?" His only solution to Larry's painful dilemma is to tie him to a chair in his room in Talbot Castle where Sir John believes he will be safe from anything. Certainly Larry's immediate success with Gwen depends in great part upon his social position. She is the daughter of an antique dealer engaged to a gamekeeper on the Talbot estate. The appeal of being sought after by Larry, "the young Master," is irresistible to her. And when Larry appears to have killed Bela the gypsy, the crime is immediately explained away by a constabulary eager to please. Larry is, then, both given an artificial sense of power because of his posi-

Talbot Castle.

tion and isolated by that position from the normal flow of life in the town. He is given to believe that he is not responsible for his actions in the same way that others are, and when he cries out for help and for understanding as he comes to realize the extent of his crimes, he is simply told by everyone to whom he speaks about it, that he is "confused." His native society diminishes his genuine and individual moral freedom and replaces it with a false freedom, which is isolative rather than individual, and destructive rather than creative.

Not only does his society betray him by offering him a static and false understanding of his moral freedom and responsibilities, but it also gives him a body of ancient and deterministic superstition with which to replace his set of personal values. The American Protestant-romantic belief in the individual's ability to change himself for the better morally and actively despite the sins of his past is replaced for Larry by the legend of lycanthropy. Both Gwen and his father recite a poem to him which emphasizes an individual's moral helplessness in the face of a fatal web of exterior circumstance:

> Even a man who is pure in heart
> And says his prayers by night
> May become a wolf when the wolfbane blooms
> And the autumn moon is bright.

The gypsy Maleva then explains the mysterious healing of the wound which he received from her son, Bela, in his wolf form, not as an emblem of freedom from the past, but as evidence of the past's power. Talbot does not become the wolf man until after she has told him that he is a werewolf. And her credo, which she speaks over the body of her son, offers only the relief of moral surrender rather than the hope of moral challenge when she says it later to Talbot: "The way you walk is thorny through no fault of your own, but as the rain enters the soil, the river enters the sea, so tears run to a predestined end. Find peace for a moment, my son."

Lawrence Talbot *is* a moral man, however, and he struggles throughout the film to do the good and to bear the responsibilities of the evil he has done, despite the lessons which the world around him offers. Bela, Maleva's son, is thoroughly a part of that world. He is a palm reader; a hand to a palmist's understanding is not primarily the instrument for change, but merely the written record of the past and an already determined future, a book of unalterable past and future history. He feels regret when he sees the pentagram, the mark of the werewolf's victim in Jennie's hand, and he warns her away, but he knows that both his regret and the

Bela knows that both his regret and
his warning are futile.

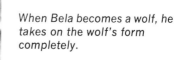

When Bela becomes a wolf, he
takes on the wolf's form
completely.

warning are futile. When he becomes a wolf, he takes on the wolf's form completely; the audience, and Lawrence Talbot, see him clearly as a four-legged beast with a tail. Talbot, who does not accept the understanding of the society he is in, struggles against the results of that way of seeing and believing. "You're insane," he tells Maleva, "Ah, quit handing me that." (The hand to Larry is not a book, but an instrument, as his verbal use of the word underlines.) And when he does give in to his own darker impulses as shaped by that society, he does not change completely. He does not become a wolf; he becomes a wolf man, the actual concrete form of the moral tension within him.

That moral tension and Talbot's struggle to resolve it positively is the source of the film's narrative structure. It is not, however, simply the struggle of a man attempting not to surrender his belief and freedom to a static determinism. His struggle is further enriched by the sexual nature of the dark force with which he must contend, a psychological force which attacks his moral strength from within as the society attacks it from without.

Lawrence Talbot, as I have said, is a physical man, although he is innocent of the full implications of his physical nature. He is a man of the senses, needing to see and touch in order to understand. He is presented to the viewer in terms of activity rather than thought, and when he does find himself forced to think abstractly, he finds it painful and useless to him. Throughout the film images of hand and foot define him to the audience. He describes himself to his father as a man who works with his hands, and his hands are expressive of his active emotional nature in other scenes. When he talks to Gwen for the first time, he handles the walking sticks and other objects in the store, and later he expresses his agony of conscience by wringing his hands and rubbing his face with them.

But even more important as an indication of Talbot's basic physical nature are the image patterns woven around his feet. The foot is a natural symbol of basic animal nature. It is an agent of motion and activity, but it is farther from the brain and less under its direct control (less flexibly useful) than the hand, and its very

The trap catches the wolf man's foot.

structure is closer to a paw than the hand or even than the foot of an ape or monkey. The foot becomes in *The Wolf Man*, a specific emblem of sexuality as well. Larry buys a walking stick from Gwen, and he offers to take her for a walk to the gypsy camp that night. The association between walking and sexuality is made explicit by Jennie's mother when she uses "walk out with" as a euphemism for sexual behavior in the scene in which she blames Talbot for the death of her daughter. Appropriately, then, when Talbot first becomes the wolf man, the foot, not the face or even the hand, is what the camera observes in the process of change. And that emphasis continues as the camera follows the wolf man's feet through the forest. When Talbot is temporarily trapped, the trap catches his foot, and when he finally dies and returns to his fully human form at the end of the film, his bare feet (as had those of Bela earlier) add strikingly to the vulnerability of his image. And, of course, when Larry awakens one morning after a night of "dreams," the muddy footprints which lead to his bed from the open window give him the proof he fears and needs of the substantiality of those dreams. No wonder that Maleva says that "The way you walk is thorny."

The emphasis on Talbot's feet would alone not justify a sexual interpretation of the film, but very much more of the texture of the film is composed of sexual imagery. Talbot is associated over and over with phallic images. The telescope through which he first sees Gwen in her bedroom is arguably phallic, and the wolf's head cane which Talbot is drawn to and purchases is clearly phallic. It is much larger and heavier than the other canes in the store, and he and Gwen use it as a central prop during their initial flirtatious banter. It is the weapon with which Larry kills the werewolf Bela, and it becomes an emblem of his physical force and potential danger to others in the film; Frank Andrews, the gamekeeper, admits that "I couldn't take my eyes off that walking stick of his." At the gypsy camp, Andrews and Talbot express their sexual rivalry for Gwen with guns in a shooting gallery, a scene clearly designed to warm any Viennese doctor's heart.

In the dark forest, Talbot's acts of violence are also presented in sexual terms. When he kills Bela, the action is framed in the open crotch of a tree, and after the struggle, Talbot staggers out of a dark hole formed by the tree. Again, this one scene would offer adequate evidence only to a confirmed Freudian, but in the later scenes in which the wolf man is stalking Gwen through the forest, she is framed more than once through the spreading crotch

When Larry kills Bela, the action is framed in the open crotch of a tree.

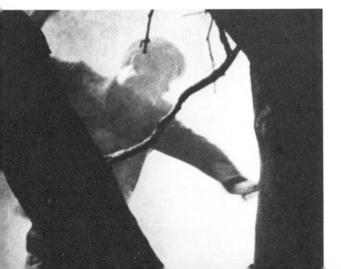

Bela, Gwen, Larry and Jennie as Bela says, "I will not disappoint you, my lady."

of a tree, and those scenes are fully sexual narratively and symbolically. Jennie's question earlier to Bela had been, "Can you tell me when I am going to be married?" It is then that Bela, who had promised that "I will not disappoint you, my lady," sees the wolfbane and recognizes that Jennie will be his victim, her marriage to be only to him in the act of death. Lawrence Talbot's story picks up that mildly sexual tone and amplifies it with his own physical vigor. In the rough hair of his wolfish form, he becomes himself an openly sexual image. His normal sexual desire has exploded into an actual figuration of lust, the archetypal beast in man, the wolf man. And his consciousness is incapable of recognizing that beast for what it is.

The brief moment of waking nightmare which Talbot has in the gypsy camp, following his talk with Maleva and his first kiss with Gwen, is strikingly similar to the sexual transformation scenes in Fleming's *Dr. Jekyll and Mr. Hyde* — a set of symbols whirling in disorder through the mind's eye. And Gwen's face is present in that nightmarish scene along with the cane, the pentagram and the other emblems of lycanthropy. Even the advertisements for the film in 1941 luridly describe Talbot as a victim of the desires of the flesh: "Not a thing, but a mortal man — a living horror with

45 /

its unearthly body a twitching tomb of strange desires . . . his hideous howl a dirge of death." What in his open American society would have been an ordinary flirtation becomes, for Lawrence Talbot, a nightmare of repressed and explosive lust in the static and closed society of his father's land. And he is rendered helpless to deal with that nightmare because his own conscience is crippled by its social context and because he is unable to see what is happening to him clearly.

Larry Talbot's courtship of Gwen Conliffe is marked from its beginning by lycanthropic imagery. The walking stick with its wolf's head and pentagram is their first topic of conversation. She recites the poem about the werewolf to him. Just as he is making overtures to see her that night, Bela passes by them on the street with the gypsy caravan. Jennie, the chaperone whom Gwen has asked to come along on the walk and whom she abandons in the camp, dies as a victim of Bela and, as her mother insists, as a victim of Larry and Gwen's lust as well. The American innocent is forced into a situation of unappeasable guilt by his own actions — actions that sprang from his innocence, his healthy physical nature, and even the moral courage which led him to kill Bela. This guilt

Larry in the forest where the mist always hangs low over the floor.

darkens his mind (his clothes grow steadily darker in tone as he sinks into his nightmare, and when he visits Gwen for the last time, the "SANEMAN" sign is obscured by shadow), and it forces him into his wolfish form and the forest in which the mist always hangs low over the floor, giving it the atmosphere of a dream. Larry is forced deeper into himself, for he finds nowhere to turn for advice in his society except to Maleva, who can offer him only "peace for a moment" and the promise of the "peace for eternity" that may be found solely in death. Larry can only cry out, "Oh, I'm sick of the whole thing," and try to bear the burden of a horror that wells out of his own inner self.

Talbot turns to his father and two other figures of rational authority in the town for help. Colonel Montford, the constable, accepts Larry's insistence that he killed a wolf and not Bela ("We'll talk to you later") all too willingly at first, because he is Sir John's son; he, too, calls him "Master Larry." The local physician, Doctor Lloyd, only offers to protect Larry from further questioning by giving him a sleeping pill. Both Montford and Lloyd assure Larry that he is confused, and Sir John amplifies their thinking when he explains to his son that he has imagined the whole thing. The werewolf, he explains, is merely "the good and evil in every man's soul" as if those forces were not capable of acting externally. "Most anything can happen," he adds, "to a man in his own mind." He suggests that Larry's mental torment may be solved by a "belief in the hereafter," a belief which Larry had already symbolically rejected in its traditional forms by leaving a church service, unable in his shame and confusion to face the curious stares of the congregation. None of the three offer Larry what he really needs, active help for a real problem. He falls back on his own strength and that strength fails; he becomes a victim of himself.

In the gypsy camp, Maleva offers Talbot a pentagram charm "to break the spell." In his emotional confusion he accepts the charm (and thereby Maleva's understanding of the ways things are), but his moral nature causes him to give it to Gwen, which offers the viewer evidence of genuine affection beyond the simple urgings of lust in his feelings for her. As his father, the society around him, and his own perception fail him, he loses moral strength and falters in his struggle with the beast within. When Gwen shows him the charm toward the end of the film, he sees in her hand the sign of the pentagram, the sign that she will be his next victim. Charms and spells are of no avail in his very real moral crisis, and he has absolutely nowhere left to turn.

A motherless son, he does turn to his father as his last resort. Sir John's only response is to tie him to a chair in his room at Talbot Castle where he may watch the planned wolf hunt that night. He ignores Larry's plea that he is the object of that hunt, and his refusal to listen marks his final betrayal of his son, for the wolf man is able easily to burst the bonds that held Larry. Larry's moral nature asserts itself one last time before his final descent into the dark abyss within him when he insists that his father take the wolf's head cane with him to the hunt. Maleva had told him earlier that "A werewolf can be killed only with a silver bullet or a silver knife or a stick with a silver handle" when she was trying to convince him that he had killed her son. Talbot's last moral act is, then, an act of love like that of giving the charm to Gwen, but it is also (again, like the gift of the charm to Gwen) an act of self-destruction.

During the carefully orchestrated hunt in the forest at the film's end, Gwen searches for Larry while the wolf man stalks her. ("I've got to find him," she tells Maleva, who replies, "Come with me or he will find you!"). But the point of view in the film, which has hitherto been strictly Larry's, has shifted, not to Gwen or Maleva, but to Sir John. Larry has fought his struggle as best he could and lost; he has made his final moral gesture. The morally active center of the film has shifted to Sir John, the most powerful figure in this society who must now see the truth of what he and it have wrought.

Sir John is upset and unsure of himself during the hunt, and he sets out alone from the shooting stand. He has told Doctor Lloyd of his tying Larry to his chair, and the doctor has accused him of being totally selfish: "Does the prestige of your family name mean more to you than your son's health?" When he meets Maleva in the dark forest, he is eager to accuse her of filling his son's head with "nonsense," and he insists that he doesn't believe her

*Sir John, now at least half sure that the wolf man is Larry,
rushes to Gwen's aid.*

witch's tales, "Not for a minute." But under her questioning, he
confesses that he is wandering away from the hunters because "I
wanted to be with my son." The wolf man soon finds Gwen and
attacks her, and Sir John, now at least half sure that it is Larry,
rushes to her aid. The wolf man attacks him, and their fight ends
with Sir John's killing his son with the silver headed cane. He, like
Larry, has now faced the darkness of "every man's soul" in its
actively physical reality.

The elements of the village and its old order close smoothly
over Larry's body at the end. Frank Andrews embraces Gwen, re-

establishing their "normal" relationship, and Colonel Montford offers to Sir John an equally soothing solution: "The wolf must have attacked her and Larry came to the rescue." But Sir John is beyond soothing; his face carries the lesson he has learned. He has seen the error of his understanding and his betrayal of his son too late, so that his participation in Larry's moral struggle comes only at its fatal end. The moral victory of Larry's final act is made manifest in his final transformation. He earned at least the right in death to be all man, to die as a human being. Maleva's last words to the dead Larry express the only other victory at the end of his struggle:

Maleva can offer Larry only the balm of peace at the end of suffering.

"Your suffering is over. Now you will find peace for eternity." Colonel Montford, who has the last operative words in the film, closes the village's eyes for the kindest of motives on the truth it may have seen. But his soothing words do not state the moral conclusion of the film, for that resides in Sir John's discovery. His world, the upper-class world safe in its book-assured understanding of the way things are, is no more. Sir John has no heir, and the vital involvement of the Talbot family in an ongoing life is at an end. The open eye of Sir John's recognition marks the moral conclusion of the film. The conclusion is, because of Sir John's being at a dead end, ironically as static and as fixed as the society and the book of the opening shots. As in *Frankenstein,* the sympathy of the audience for the figure of horror is important, but the shift of point of view to Sir John diminishes the impact of that sympathy. The film becomes Sir John's whose life is at a close, while *Frankenstein,* despite the Baron's noncomprehending good cheer, remains Henry Frankenstein's whose life with Elizabeth is at a beginning.

The Wolf Man proves upon close examination to have a complexity of form and matter which make it tempting to conclude that the cause of its relative esthetic failure is simply that it hasn't been undersood, but even with a fuller understanding of the film than a casual viewing would afford, it remains somehow unsatisfactory. And I have come to believe that the key to its failure may be found in that closed quality of its conclusion.

In part, the trouble is that the film does not try for the largeness of purpose of *Frankenstein;* it is humanistic rather than cosmic in its themes. Henry Frankenstein and his monster both reach for the light in the fullest metaphysical sense of *light.* Lawrence Talbot reaches simply for happiness, for something he can hold, his simple individual identity. Frankenstein deals with the great ray, the light beyond seeing; Larry Talbot admits his inability to understand or deal with "these things you can't even touch." His failure is not, then, so large nor so enlightening. It is too akin to the man down the street who can't stop smoking even though he has emphysema. But that explanation will not finally suffice. Lawrence Talbot's struggle does have a nobility to it even as it turns to self-destruction as the only antidote for his weakness, and the shift of point of view to Sir John at the end indicates that the film's failures as well as moral conclusion must be sought elsewhere than in the character of Lawrence Talbot.

The problem lies finally in a discord between medium and matter in the film. Among the natural qualities of the cinema as a medium are flowing motion and an open play of light. If a film is thematically closed or static, its director must work consciously against the grain of his medium. The famous freeze frame of Truffaut's closing shot in *The 400 Blows (Les Quatre Cents Coups)*, the disjointed cutting and intermittent use of sound in Godard's *Vivre sa Vie*, and the long static shots of Bergman's *Winter Light (Nattvardsgästerna)* are all careful matings of cinematic matter to the films' thematic concerns. *The Wolf Man* is a flowing film. Its texture darkens as it moves along, but its rhythm is insistently flowing, musical; even the ground seems fluid in the clinging fog of the closing forest scenes. There are practically no static shots in the film, and the flow of Ted Kent's editing supported by Charles Previn's musical score is appropriate to Larry's active nature and to the foot imagery in the film. But it does not prepare for or allow the thematic closure at the end. Maleva's repeated insistence that all flowing finds a static end simply does not do the job; the rain's entering the soil is simply not a proper metaphorical equivalent for the finality of such a death ("peace for all eternity") or such a moral dead end. *Frankenstein*'s artificial sets and its structural verticality both prepare an ending that is fabular and destructive, but they work in harmony with the film's steady rhythmic progress and its overt dependence upon light as theme and substance to prepare for the rich ambiguity of the film's ending and its openness. The structural and textural elements of *The Wolf Man* do not work harmoniously toward an open end, but neither do they work harmoniously toward the film's thematic closed end. Certainly the developing darkness, the increasing hysteria of Chaney's performance, the shift of point of view to Sir John, and Claude Rains' rigidly controlled performance were attempts on Waggner's part to shape his medium to his matter, but they simply lack the radical strength to countermand the movement of the rest of the film.

The Wolf Man is, however, a film worthy of careful consideration. It expresses the horror of a man's loss of self-control and finally his loss of self. Its themes hold their validity, and its images are still able to grip the imagination. Curt Siodmak may have imposed a closed European theme on Waggner's open and flowing American style, or possibly Waggner did not fully grasp the implications of Siodmak's screenplay and shape his film fully to it. But, in either case, they did produce a carefully wrought if flawed film of considerable integrity and of a haunting darkness which deserves far better than it has received at the hands of its few critics.

NIGHT OF THE LIVING DEAD:
"IT'S NOT LIKE JUST A WIND THAT'S PASSING THROUGH."

Night of the Living Dead is in many ways a unique film. A low budget ($114,000 by George Romero's accounting) production, the first feature length film of a group of independent filmmakers in Pittsburgh, released on the drive-in circuit with no fanfare, it has managed to become a striking commercial success — according to Paul McCullough, "*the most profitable* horror film ever to be produced outside the walls of a major studio." Lines stretched around the block in so unlikely a city as Barcelona, and the *Wall Street Journal* reported that it was the top money-making film in all of Europe in the year of its release. In this country, it gained a large and committed audience and a rising critical reputation, so much so that the film department of the Museum of Modern Art invited Romero to present it in a showing at the museum as part of a series devoted to the work of significant new directors.

The easiest explanation of the film's popular success would be to say that it has simply outdone all of its rivals in the lingering and gross detail of its scenes of violence and that its appeal has simply been to that basest of needs, the need for unrestrained violence. This is the explanation favored by the *Reader's Digest*, which ran an article denouncing the film for its bad influence on

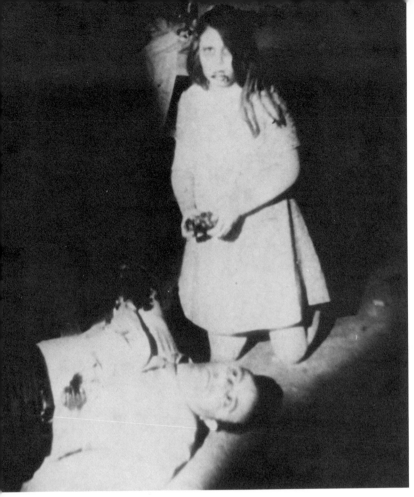

In **Night of the Living Dead**, Karen devours her father's arm.

the minds of children, and of *Variety*, where an early review of the film found that it "casts serious aspersions on the integrity of its makers, distrib Walter Reade, the film industry as a whole and exhibs who book the pic, as well as raising doubts about the future of the regional film movement and the moral health of filmgoers who cheerfully opt for unrelieved sadism." And even the film's admirers were forced to admit that it is an example of "grainy Grand Guignol" and that it possesses a "gluey, bottomless horror." The film's horrific specifics are remarkably detailed — walking corpses fighting over and eating the intestines of the film's young

lovers, a closeshot of one of them eating her hand, a child's stab-
bing of her mother on camera fourteen times or gnawing on her
father's severed arm, to say nothing of the countless re-killings of
the living dead, the bashing in of their skulls. One of the film's
backers was in the meat-packing business, and its footage shows
much evidence of his enthusiastic support. In fact, films like *The
Texas Chain Saw Massacre* which have followed *Night of the Living
Dead* are now being referred to by critics like Lew Brighton as
"meat movies."

Certainly the film's open-eyed detailing of human taboos,
murder and cannibalism, have had much to do with its success.
What girl hasn't, at one time or another, wished to kill her mother?
Karen, in this film, offers a particularly vivid opportunity to commit
the forbidden deed vicariously. And what brother hasn't wished to
devour his younger sister, sexually or otherwise, at least once?
But the film takes the source of its horrors from another desire
and a fear that lies certainly as deep in the human consciousness,
if not deeper. This is a fear of the dead and particularly of the
known dead, of dead kindred. Anthony Masters reports in *The
Natural History of the Vampire* on some of the primitive ritual in-
volving that fear in his study of the vampire:

> *It was always absolutely essential to speed the spirit on
> its way once death had taken place. At all costs the late
> departed must join the family's ancestors without delay.
> Should there be a delay the spirit would take offense,
> would hover malignantly around and when it did reach
> its eventual destination would have singled out default-
> ing members of the family for retribution. Precautions
> for the spirit's escape include the opening of windows
> and doors, the putting out of the fire in the hearth (in
> case the spirit doggedly refused conventional exits and
> insisted on the chimney), and keeping careful watch on
> the corpse.*

The film is almost a reenactment of these rituals in reverse. The
unburied recent dead stalk the landscape seeking the flesh of the
living, and the only defense against them is the shutting of doors

The unburied recent dead stalk the landscape seeking
the flesh of the living.

and windows and the use of fire as a barricade. All traditional
methods of handling the fact of death fail; as Doctor Grimes puts
it in the film, "The bereaved will have to forego the dubious
comforts that a funeral service can give." The ancient fear is unleashed on the characters in the film and on the audience with a
force that only savage violence can repel. The movie thrusts its
audience into a situation of primordial fear and offers them neither
rational nor religious relief. The apparently universal human ability
to find pleasure in an artistic rehearsing of its worst fears is certainly at the heart of the film's popular success, and the film's
unrelenting avoidance of all traditional ways of handling the fear it
has called up must be as much at the heart of its critical success.

But the question of what the film really *is*, of its esthetic
identity, is poorly served by either of these answers. It is not simply
a film which is more frightening (or disgusting) than its competi-
tion, because it has an impact that other films with just as much
gore do not have, and that impact must be found in the film's
successful expression of a fear even deeper than the overt fear of

the dead. And its admiring critics have not managed to explain just what the film does *do* even as it rejects the traditional approaches to its themes and subject matter. Elliott Stein sees the film's horror and violence as an exaggeration in kind of that in *Patton*, and he goes on to equate both the living dead and the posse which hunts them down, "all of them so horrifying, so convincing, who mow down, defoliate and gobble up everything in their path," with "ordinary people, in all the trance-like security of their 'silent majority.' " In other words, he explains the film, as his use of *defoliate* is intended to indicate, in terms of the familiar political rhetoric of the later 1960s and thereby sells the film short. Joseph Lewis takes much the same position when he describes the film's impact as "cathartic for us, who forget about the horrors around us which aren't, alas, movies," and goes on to say that LBJ might never "have permitted the napalming of the Vietnamese" had he seen *Night of the Living Dead* (a view which David Pirie supports by saying that the film "manages to bring us closer to the question of American involvement in Vietnam and racism than any of the recent documentary-type features which tackle such issues head-on"). But the horror of war and a disapproval and fear of the American middle class do not, for all their being related to the central fear and horror of the film, explain it adequately. For, if that were the case, a newsreel, on the one hand, and Nathanael West's *The Day of the Locust*, on the other, would be esthetic equivalents of *Night of the Living Dead*, and they simply aren't.

Richard McGuinness avoids the stock political response in his review of the film in *The Village Voice*, and he comes much closer to the film's real values when he praises its "crudely accomplished but spontaneous effect," its "manic overacting," the plot which "is unrestrained and incorrigibly kills all the characters in what, near the end, becomes an avalanche of atrocities," and the fatally attacked Helen's "shrieking inertia" which "happens simply because . . . things are so demonstrably bad, life is no longer desirable." He stops short, however, and turns from the film's unique qualities to praise it for its narrative technique: "These fervently acted out, numerous unpremeditated cruelties in the midst of situations already at an intolerable level resemble the comic building in silent movies; and [*Night of the Living Dead*] by its daring crudeness and while scaring the pants off the audience, rediscovers the silent art of story-telling."

Before these strands of McGuinness's reading of the film can be pressed convincingly on to their proper conclusion, an examination of *Night of the Living Dead*'s textural and structural elements is in order. Although it is a film radically different in kind from either *Frankenstein* or *The Wolf Man*, it is as thoroughly and carefully composed, and the nature of its composition is the key to its thematic and esthetic values, to its moral nature.

The essential quality of the film's setting and of its characters is their ordinary nature. The graveyard in the film's opening scenes and the house where the rest of the film takes place offer an immediate and telling contrast with *Frankenstein, The Wolf Man* and almost all of the American horror films of the 1930s and 1940s. Even the cheap horror films of the 1950s (*I Was a Teenage Werewolf, I Was a Teenage Frankenstein, Frankenstein's Daughter*), with all their insistence upon the everyday availability of their horrors, have a slick, adolescent, greasy glamour that seems flashy and fantastic compared with the dully commonplace settings of *Night of the Living Dead*. The graveyard is no neo-expressionistic set like that of *Frankenstein* with a painted sky and lighting that comments on the scene even as it functions within it; it is a small Pennsylvania country graveyard, flatly lit and unretouched. (I recently ran across a viewer who had the added horror of seeing one of the living dead lurch across his mother's grave.) And the house is an ordinary frame farm house, no book-filled castle overlooking the perpetually befogged forest of Lawrence Talbot's mind.

The night of the living dead is a Sunday night, the first after the time change in the early spring. The season, with its overtones of temporarily dead nature and lingering winter cold, is symbolically significant, as is the Sunday, which emphasizes the failure of religion in a secular age. Johnny, the first victim of the living dead in the film, admits to his sister Barbara that "There's not much sense in my going to church," and the film offers no evidence to contradict him. Beyond these rudimentary symbolic uses of the setting, there is no further use of the landscape except in its ordinariness. Its bleak emptiness suggests the frailty and the hopelessness of the characters' situation, but it is no desert or polar ice cap — just ordinary, familiar western Pennsylvania countryside.

The farmhouse has its symbolic uses, too, but they are minimal. There are in one of its rooms several mounted animal heads, innocent enough in themselves, but which do take on certain symbolic overtones in the context of the equally dead but moving human figures around the house and the posse with its hunting rifles. But Romero's only functional use of these heads is for a cheap shock (one of the very few in the film that isn't genuinely integral to its narrative flow) when Barbara first enters the house. There is also a small music box with revolving mirrors which sounds, for one brief, lyrically photographed scene, a sad little note of beauty and sanity in a context of madness. But that scene, too, is actually out of place tonally in the film, despite the hollow loveliness of the tune and the pathetic fragility of the tiny instrument, its turning mirrors reflecting only themselves. The rest of the house is symbolic only in its functional uses. Its simple, daily, practical nature is transformed by necessity into that of a fortress, a last barrier against the forces of destruction, and the ease with which it gives itself to that transformation offers some symbolic comment on its always having been such a fortress even in its peaceful past. The cellar also gains a symbolic quality from its structural use in the film's narrative. But, otherwise, the house is a house — ordinary and real, practically unchanged by the filmmakers, symbolizing and meaning only itself.

Even the specific tonal quality of the image is ordinary. Although Romero says that the use of black and white was "a budgetary decision," Elliott Stein says that "Romero was offered a budget for color; he preferred shooting in black and white; the result is a flat murky ambience which is perfect for the ramshackle American gothic landscape where the events occur." Save for some echoes early in the film of the Dutch angles of Whale's *Bride of Frankenstein*, the photography calls attention to itself, appropriately like the setting, only in its ordinariness. This ordinary quality is no confession on Romero's part of inadequacies of budget or of ability. He has chosen a photographic style to suit his setting, and he has chosen a setting which is essential to his thematic concerns.

The characters (the living characters) are just as ordinary. Stein is correct, whatever his reasons, in identifying these people with the American middle class, the "silent majority." A sociologist might worry about classifying some of them higher or lower, but they are indisputably ordinary people. There is no scientist here dreaming of the great ray, nor any wise gypsy ministering to spiritual hurt, no barons or knights. The scene is American, and the characters are democratically ordinary and American. Perhaps the only unusual thing about them is that no one of them ever comments about one of their number's being black, especially in the light of his assuming a natural leadership. But even that lack of race prejudice in a tight situation may be more ordinarily American than we might suspect.

Barbara and Johnny, the first characters to appear in the film, are two ordinary young people on their way to place a wreath on their father's grave, unconsciously acting out an ancient ritual of ancestor worship and also of propitiation to the fearful dead. Barbara takes it seriously, but Johnny doesn't. He is a very modern and urban young man. When she kneels to say a prayer, he says, "Praying's for church, huh?" When he notices her uneasiness in the increasingly dusky cemetery, he frightens her — "They're coming for you Barbara" — his voice an imitation of Karloff's familiar horror film tones. There is nothing particularly cruel or unusual in his behavior; he has always tried to frighten Barbara, and he remembers how their grandfather had warned him that he'd be "damn't to hell" for doing it. He is not a particularly sensitive or pleasant fellow, but when the first living deadman appears, he struggles with him manfully and gives his life to save his sister. Barbara manages to escape, but when she reaches the house and accepts the protection of Ben, she retreats further into a state of shocked unawareness, into an amniotic inner self. Both of them are ordinary, "realistic" people, and they both respond in normal ways — Johnny mocks his sister but gives his life for her, and

When the first living deadman appears, Johnny struggles with him manfully.

Barbara finds the strength to escape a danger, but her strength gives out abruptly and naturally when she finds some semblance of sanctuary.

The other characters who congregate in the besieged house are as familiar and as ordinary. Ben, the black "hero" of the film, is a working man. He is good with his hands, and it is he who turns the house into a fortress. He is also the most articulate and, to all appearances, the most intelligent of the people in the house; his long speech, which is the first indication of the scope of what is happening and which he delivers as he works purposefully to

Ben and Barbara.

shore up the house's natural defenses, establishes him as a man who is fully capable of active thought and rational action. But, again, his heroic potential is shown in an ordinary context; he is just an intelligent and vital man caught in bad circumstances, trying to do what he can about it.

The Cooper family, Harry, Helen and their daughter Karen, are even more familiar. Far from heroic, Harry Cooper is nevertheless a strong man, but one whose strength expresses itself in abrasive

The Coopers are a relatively typical modern family.

opinion and nearly hysterical action. His response to the situation is to hide in the cellar and wait until the problem goes away by itself or is handled by someone else. His selfish certainty gives him a strength almost equal to Ben's rational activism, and their clash, ideological and personal, gives the center of the film its tension. Helen is an intelligent but bitter woman. Her marriage is a burden to her, and she appears to endure it only for the sake of her daughter. Her desire to save the child gives her the strength to use her bitterness as a weapon against her husband. "We may not enjoy living together," she tells him at one point, "but dying together isn't going to solve anything." The child is ill, having been bitten by one of the living dead, but seems otherwise to be a reasonable, normal child. They are, in brief, a relatively typical modern family, if we are to believe the divorce statistics, living only by negative values, bitter and abrasive toward each other and others, separated from hysteria and violence only by a thin veneer of social necessity.

The two other characters in the house would have been the romantic hero and heroine if this had been a 1950s teenage horror film. Tom and Judy are a young couple, not yet married but very much in love. They are a simple pair, lacking the forcefulness of either Ben or Harry, but they do offer a contrast to the Coopers' failed marriage. "You always have a smile for me," Tom tells Judy, and her loyalty to him is strong enough to impel her to risk danger with him when he and Ben try to gas up the truck for an escape. They are, almost embarrassingly, typical teenage lovers — not very intelligent but genuinely in love.

The sheriff is a grotesque figure, but he and his posse are at least typical of a modern American image of what they should be, if they are somewhat exaggerated for the real thing. The posse is composed of residents of the area where the film was being shot, and they have all the authenticity of a newsreel. To add to that authenticity, the newscaster covering the posse's activity is simply playing himself — Bill "Chilly Billy" Caudille, a Pittsburgh television newscaster and host of a late night horror film show. In fact, the only two professional actors in the whole film are Duane Jones (Ben) and Judith O'Dea (Barbara). Both co-producers play roles (Russell Streiner as Johnny and Karl Hardman as Harry), but neither of them is a professional actor. The film is, then, the story of everyday people in an ordinary landscape, played by everyday people who are, for the most part, from that ordinary locale. The way in which *Night of the Living Dead* transforms that familiar and ordinary world into a landscape of unrelenting horror reveals the film's moral nature and the deep and terrible fear which is at its heart.

The living dead themselves are the active and catalytic agency for the release of all of the film's horrors. The idea of the dead's return to a kind of life and their assault on the living is no new idea; it is present in all the ancient tales of vampires and ghouls and zombies, and it has been no stranger to films. *Night of the Living Dead* derives from those countless tales and films and more specifically, as Romero has confessed in his preface to the "novelization" of the film, to Richard Matheson's novel *I Am Legend*. And, as Calvin Thomas Beck pointed out in his article on the film in *Castle of Frankenstein*, it shares very striking similarities to *Invisible Invaders* and to *The Last Man on Earth*, which was based on *I Am Legend*, and we might add *The Omega Man*, which was also based on Matheson's novel. David Pirie suggests that John Gilling's *Plague of the Zombies* "seems to have been one of the secondary influences behind Romero's fascinating American nightmare." All of these tales and films spring from that ancient fear of the dead, and that fear is the first upon which *Night of the Living Dead* touches.

The scene in the graveyard is based purely on the fear the living have of the dead. A certain amount of graveyard fear does spring from its forceful reminder of the universality and inevitability of human death, but a literal fear of the dead themselves does still exist in the most placid of human hearts. Johnny frightens Barbara with that fear, and it is the fear that the audience feels throughout that scene and up to the point at which Ben kills the living deadman in the house. The effectiveness of the dead woman at the top of the stairs depends upon that fear. But after Ben shows that the dead can be killed again, the fear of the dead begins to lose power. The dead, unlike death itself, can be stopped and become a more ordinary horror, one to which there can be a practical response.

When the information about the living dead begins to be available, by direct experience and the radio and the television news reports, the ancient fear of the dead is dispelled almost totally. The living dead are revealed to be neither supernatural in origin nor impelled by ideas of revenge upon the living. Triggered by radiation brought to earth accidentally by a Venus probe, the recently dead have arisen and attacked the living for no motive whatsoever other than a blind need for food. They have no identities and are really no different from any other natural disaster; Tom specifically compares them to a flood, and he is right. They are, as Doctor Grimes puts it, "dangerous," but they are "just dead flesh." Once their individuality is denied, they become no less dangerous, but they do lose that initial aura of ancient fear. They become, in a word, ordinary. "Beat 'em or burn 'em," the sheriff says, "they go up pretty easy." And he expresses the loss of that aura of fear most fully when he says, "Yeah, they're dead; they're all messed up."

As the traditional fear of the dead loses its force in the film, it is replaced by another fear, one less easily defined and far more difficult to overcome once it has been established. The dead characters in the film, like the living ones, are very ordinary people — distorted by death and the artificial life in them, but still recog-

The dead are very ordinary people.

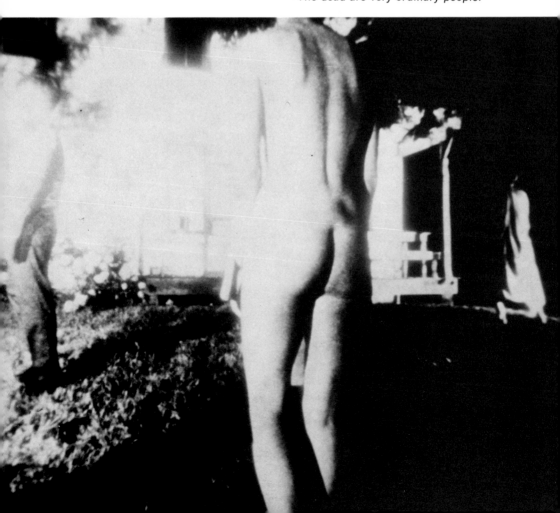

nizably ordinary. Some of them are fully dressed; one of them is rather fat and dressed only in jockey shorts; one of them, a young woman, is naked. They look vulnerable, and they are vulnerable, to a blow to the head and to fire. As their danger becomes more ordinary in the film, the other fear reveals itself. The living people are dangerous to each other, both because they are potentially living dead should they die and because they are human with all of the ordinary human failings. Ben kills Harry because his cowardice has risked Ben's life, and the clash of egos between Ben and Harry endanger the lives of all the others throughout the film. But even more frightening than that familiar danger is yet another one — the danger of the whole ordinary world itself.

Tom and Judy die because they courageously dare to try to make the truck an instrument of escape, but they die also because Judy gets caught in the truck, and, as Tom tries to free her, the truck explodes. They die, in other words, because accidents do happen and because gas does explode when touched by fire. The living dead die again because the ordinary world may be turned into such an effective weapon. An innocent farmhouse becomes a quite formidable engine of war. Not only do knives and guns exercise a dangerous role in the film, but gasoline and old bottles and rags do as well, and table legs and hammers, a garden trowel and even a stuffed chair used as a flaming torch. Either by the action of accident or by that of human purposiveness, the ordinary, everyday world may become dangerous and deadly. Barbara jumps in fright when she sees the stuffed animal heads, and then she and the audience relax as they realize there is no danger in these inanimate things. But by the end of the film, not only have all of the human beings in it become dangerous to each other, but the familiar household objects around them have become as dangerous. The traditional fear of the dead sensitizes the audience to fear at the beginning of the film, but by its end, that audience has been exposed to a much deeper and more powerful fear — the fear of life itself.

Night of the Living Dead establishes the fear of the ordinary and of life itself with great skill, but even that does not give the film its especial quality. For, after all, that fear has been expressed and examined and resolved countless times before. It is Kierkegaard's sickness unto death or Poe's fever called living or Sartre's nausea pressed to its extreme; ways, both religious and secular, have been devised for its cure, and much of the greatest art of our culture has been an expression of that fear and of its vital resolution. The essential nature of *Night of the Living Dead* may be found in the way it resolves that fear which it has called up, in the textural and structural mode of that resolution — which proves to be finally less a resolution than a surrender to (and even a celebration of) the fear itself.

The film is primarily one of ceaseless and unremitting struggle, a struggle for survival. Its structural design is one of closing in; its plot is built upon that design, and its texture fills out that narrative and structural form.

The plot is really a simple one. Because of an accidental introduction of harmful radiation into the earth's atmosphere, the recent and unburied dead become activated into a semblance of life (albeit unconscious and undividuated), and they attack the living for food. A group of people (three men, three women and a child) seek shelter in an isolated farmhouse. There they struggle for their lives. Some of them respond to the challenge rationally and bravely. One of them responds with hysteria and cowardice. One retreats from the fight into a state of shock. All of them are killed, either by the living dead or by each other, except for one; he is killed by the posse who assume him to be one of the living dead. Within that simple plot line, the characters exhibit traditional virtues and vices, but the good and the bad, the innocent and the guilty, all suffer the same fate; they all lose. In fact, those virtues which have been the mainstay of our civilized history seem to lead to defeat in this film even more surely than the traditional vices. Helen Cooper dies because her mother's love for her daughter renders her incapable of defending herself against the child's ghoulish attack. Tom and Judy die because they have the courage to try to help the whole group escape and because they love each other. Barbara dies because she snaps out of her moral lethargy and goes to the aid of Helen Cooper at the door; there she sees her brother Johnny, now one of the living dead, and is carried away to her

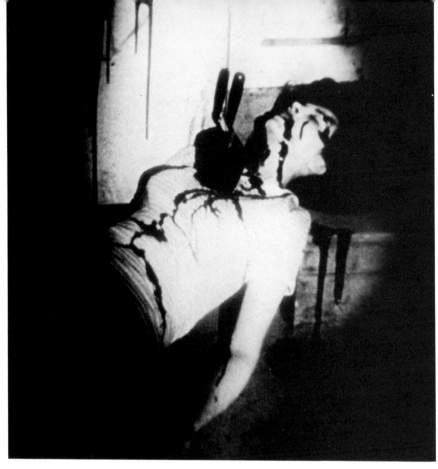

*Helen Cooper dies because her motherly love renders her
incapable of defending herself.*

death by him. Ben, whose strength and reason keep the group functioning as long as possible, sees all of his ideas fail and prove destructive, finds himself driven by rage to kill one of his fellow living men, and ends by retreating into the very cellar that his reason had earlier branded "a death trap." His death at the hands of the posse is only the final blow of a long series that have been slowly draining the life from him throughout the film.

The plot is, then, one of simple negation, an orchestrated descent to death in which all efforts toward life fail. As Romero puts it, "The film opens with a situation that has already disintegrated to a point of little hope, and it moves progressively toward

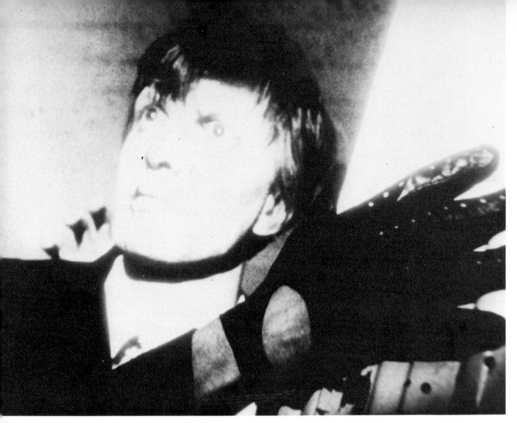

Johnny is now one of the living dead.

absolute despair and ultimate tragedy. Nobody comes riding in at the end with the secret formula that will save us all. The ghouls, in essence, win out."

The texture of the film fills out that negative narrative form. Elliott Stein has pointed out how the film is "a symphony of psychotic hands — the house is surrounded by endless rows of ghastly grasping insatiable claws which poke through boarded windows and seize victims whose own hands are munched like hand-burghers." The hand, that most active and productive physical extension of the human mind, is rendered perversely in this film; its values are inverted. At first, Ben is given to the viewer very much in terms of his hands — he rebuilds the house with them, he strikes Barbara to end her hysteria with his hand, he drags the body of the old lady away with his hands, he kills the first of the living dead to enter the house by hand, he covers Barbara's feet with shoes

Barbara's defeat in ''a symphony of psychotic hands.''

he has found for her (shielding their vulnerable bareness and offering her at least the appearance of the normal, of rational control). But as the film progresses, the futility of his manual efforts becomes increasingly apparent; the hand loses practical and symbolic power. His slapping of Barbara snaps her out of her hysteria but into a near coma. He is forced to turn to the rifle rather than the hand as the emblem of his power and the extension of his will. When the first ghoul's hand bursts through his handiwork (the boarded window), it signals the beginning of the end, the descent into Stein's "symphony of psychotic hands," the inexorable movement away from reason and value into mindless terror and loss of meaning. The eating of Judy's hand marks the final defeat of the hand as an effective emblem of rational and moral behavior.

73 /

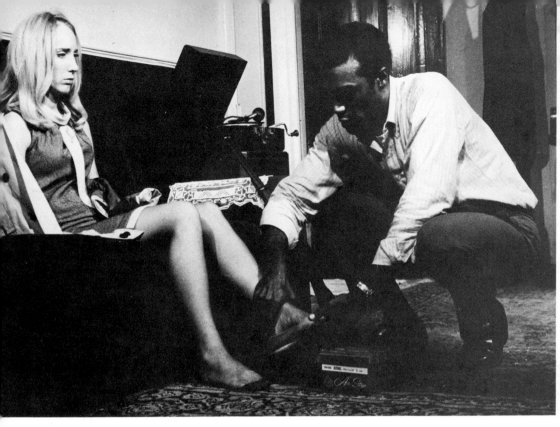

Ben covers Barbara's feet with shoes that he has found.

The structural system of closing in is formed of three elements. The simplest of these is the visual textural and traditionally symbolic use of light. The film's movement is a traditional one in Western narrative and especially in horror films; it moves from waning daylight through a night of horror to a new dawn — the familiar structure of "Night on Bald Mountain," or, for that matter, St. John of the Cross's dark night of the soul. But *Night of the Living Dead* transforms that pattern by imposing fire into it. The movement from daylight into night is clear enough; dusk and the first of the living dead arrive at the same time. Electric light and fire cooperate during the early part of the night as tools of the human struggle for survival, but the electric light finally fails and the fire takes on a dangerous force out of human control. Tom and Judy die by fire, and, by the light of the new day, Ben's body is thrown finally on a pyre and burned.

The geographical structure of the film is, like *Frankenstein*, vertical, but with a radical simplicity completely different from that film's structural ambiguity and complexity. The movement of the film is down and in. It opens on a car climbing a hill to a cemetery in the daylight. As the light fails and the living dead appear, it moves downhill with Barbara as she flees to the house. There, in the surrounded house, Ben fights against a further descent and for traditional human values. When Harry Cooper insists that "The

Ben is carried to the makeshift funeral pyre.

cellar is the strongest place," Ben replies that "The cellar is a death trap." "You can be boss down there," he continues, "I'm boss up here." But Ben's conviction that "They can't get in here" depends upon strict communal cooperation, and when that co-operation fails, Ben himself descends into the cellar where he is ironically as safe as Cooper insisted he would be. But he descends even deeper than the cellar; he descends into the neuronic depths of himself, into a dark and primitive past without reason or light, only fear and hopelessness. After killing Harry Cooper once again (this time as one of the living dead, trying to rise again with the bloody stump of his arm waving feebly in the air — a grotesque parody of the promise of Christian resurrection) and the reactivated Helen Cooper, Ben, the articulate man, becomes completely silent; he upsets a table, turns around the room moving things aimlessly, and finally crouches with his gun in the dark corner of the cellar — hopelessly and permanently gone to earth.

There is, of course, a final ascent for Ben, but it is no more a counteraction of the descending structure of the film than is the dawn's light an effective counter to the fire's power. He climbs upstairs, still silent, his gun at the ready, and stares blankly at the posse crossing the field. But he is not the Ben who struggled so bravely through the night; that Ben was lost forever in the lightless cellar. His ascent ends only in his death, and the sheriff is symbol-ically accurate when he defines Ben simply as "That's another one for the fire." He has lost even the struggle for simple identity that Lawrence Talbot at least won by his death. Ben is carried with his head hanging down to the makeshift funeral pyre and burned, and this marks the end of his personal physical descent from a man on his feet throughout most of the film to the crouching figure of fear in the cellar to this limp and lifeless sprawl in the flames.

The third parallel structural element is the film's editing. Romero, who also cut the film, did not make Waggner's mistake of underestimating the positive force of the moving medium of cinema. The editing throughout is fully supportive and expressive of the film's thematic, textural and structural design. The film opens with a long shot of the car moving through the Pennsylvania countryside, a lyrical shot were it not for the bareness of the black and white image. The cutting is simple and conventional, even during the struggle with and flight from the first of the living dead, although the use of the neo-Whale angles begins to appear. After the shock cuts when Barbara enters the house and starts at the animal heads, the film moves into its longest speech (Ben's account of his experiences) which Romero keeps alive by supporting Ben's articulate account with a smoothly and rationally edited sequence of shots of Ben using his hands (and head, figuratively) to barricade the house. After the discovery of the Coopers, Judy and Tom in the cellar, the film's cutting becomes increasingly nervous and agitated, easing off occasionally but never losing its increasing speed. After the deaths of Tom and Judy, the film's pacing becomes as frenetic as its action, subsiding only as Ben retreats into the cellar as the living dead stumble aimlessly about overhead.

The coming of dawn and the posse is handled very smoothly and simply; the editing supports the symbolic use of the dawn light — both indicate the reestablishment of human and rational order in the chaotic situation. But Romero undercuts the steady motion of the film just as he does the light. After Ben's death, he abruptly shatters the film's smooth forward motion. The account of the burning of Ben is composed of very grainy still shots with high-level voice overs, connected still to the narrative flow, but disjointedly and in fragments. After shattering the naturally vital force of the medium with these devices, Romero moves one step further, perverting its motion by forcing it to serve the negative symbolic force of the fire. The film moves one last time out of those grainy stills into clarity and motion, but that last moving image in the film is of the fire, devouring the hero's body and imposing its destructive light on the living light of the day.

Richard McGuinness suggests that "Studded throughout the comic book dread and brought to its service are many situational motifs from Hitchcock movies and several bits of well-integrated Hitchcock technique." But he adds that "The Hitchcock aspects are shorn of their evasive, level-hopping, metaphysic-implying obfuscations and work simply to increase dread." Romero does use Hitchcock's devices "simply to increase dread," but that use itself expresses a metaphysical position. Despite its similarities to the novel *I Am Legend* and the films *The Last Man on Earth, Invisible Invaders, The Omega Man* and *Plague of the Zombies*, the artistic antecedent for *Night of the Living Dead* is most clearly Hitchcock's *The Birds*. In both films, a group of people are besieged by an apparently harmless and ordinary world gone beserk, struggle to defend themselves against the danger, and struggle to maintain their rationality and their values at the same time. The similarities are interesting, but the differences are more revealing.

Hitchcock's colorful and highly artificial (in the fullest artistic sense) film is a parable of human existence in the face of a dangerous and, more importantly, inexplicable and mysterious world. In it, the characters are saved from that menace because of their rational efforts, but also because the world stops trying to kill them for the moment. Romero's consciously real and ordinary world is just as dangerous, but it is neither inexplicable nor mysterious. Its menace has a rational explanation (the radiation) that Hitchcock's birds do not, and its characters die because they are inhabitants of a world of blind and deadly chance. This world of chance may be meaningless, but its meaninglessness is its own explanation. The end of *The Birds* opens out (as does the last shot) to a sunlit world which is dangerous and inexplicable, but at the same time beautiful and awesome; *Night of the Living Dead* closes in to death and fire, both rendered in black and white, both implying a finality which is neither beautiful nor awesome, but merely ugly and cheap.

Even if Hitchcock had closed his film differently and used the static and closed shot which he claims, in Peter Bogdanovich's *The Cinema of Alfred Hitchcock*, to have "toyed with" (a shot of their arrival in San Francisco, the scene of safety, "lap-dissolving on them in the car, looking, and there is the Golden Gate Bridge — covered in birds"), *The Birds* would still have been radically different from *Night of the Living Dead*, because its values would still have been ongoing. Its central characters develop and change for the better in its course; they maintain their values to the end, as exemplified by the young girl's taking of the love birds with her; they grow within themselves and in relation to each other. And the audience would still have been left, not with a fear of the ordinary and of life, but with a fearful sense of its largeness and its unfathomable mystery. Hitchcock's rich and positive use of the medium and all of its artifices simply would not have produced the ending and the values of *Night of the Living Dead*.

Romero's film is much closer to the nihilistic strain in the films of Roman Polanski; its ending repeats in its own terms and in dead seriousness the comically anarchistic ending of *The Fearless Vampire Killers*, and Ivan Butler's description of the horrific aspects of *Rosemary's Baby* (a film of which Polanski himself does not approve) could well be applied to *Night of the Living Dead*: "the menace of the everyday, above all the hidden, deeprooted fears in all of us, the unfaced awful possibilities we all 'know' could become reality — the nerve-ends themselves are touched with a cold finger." But, in fact, *Rosemary's Baby*, in which the devil is born into the world incarnate, has more magnitude and possibility than *Night of the Living Dead*. It at least expresses a belief in and a sense of something powerfully larger than a meaningless world

The posse and its random killing of Ben diminishes life and all human possibility and value.

of chance, even if that something is the embodiment of super-natural evil; the existence of Satan does imply the existence of God, and the tawdry silliness of the devil's disciples, despite their immediate success, does offer at least the hope of further opposi-tion to evil. *Night of the Living Dead*, however, expresses only human smallness and ineffectuality. The posse at the end, with its lack of feeling, ("Somebody's had a cookout here, Vince," the sheriff says when he finds the burned out truck in which Tom and Judy died) — that posse and its random killing of Ben diminishes life and all of human possibility and value as much as the birth of Satan's son and more than any of the trick reverse endings of the new wave of horror films (*House of Dark Shadows*, *The Return of Count Yorga*, *The Velvet Vampire*), because it reduces life and its values to a nearly absolute minimum.

The real horror of *Night of the Living Dead* is not, then, a result of its inspiring a fear of the dead or even a fear of the ordi-nary world. It lies rather in its refusal to resolve those fears in any way that does not sacrifice human dignity and human value. The deaths in the film are all to no purpose; they do not finally serve the practical cause of survival, nor do they act to the enhancement of larger human value. When someone dies, his values die with him. The audience may feel at the film's end a certain sympathy for Ben, because of his attempts to maintain his values, but that sympathy lingers from the audience's preconceptions and not from the film proper. Ben loses his moral struggle as well as his prac-tical one for survival; he surrenders to the darkness in himself and to that around him. Unlike Lawrence Talbot, he has no silver cane to pass on, for he has no values left.

The film as a whole undercuts most of the cherished values of our whole civilization, what Faulkner called "the eternal verities." It ridicules government in the scenes in Washington, which seem to be left over from a Marx Brothers movie, but more seriously it casts the whole rule of law into doubt with the territorial disputes inside the house and their final resolution in violence with the death of Harry Cooper. Courage is shown throughout to lead only to death. The idea of the family is perhaps more harshly assaulted than any other in the film. The Coopers snarl at each other, and their daughter finally kills her mother and partially devours her father. Family ties actually become dangerous in the film — Helen does not even try to save herself from her daughter because the idea of familial love was so deeply ingrained in her, and Barbara allows herself to be taken out by Johnny and the other ghouls because of the same idea and the shock of having it shattered. Love itself comes to nothing but a fiery end, as Tom and Judy's experience shows. Even the value of individual identity collapses as it reveals itself to be weak in the face of disaster, even weaker in one respect than the body, which is able to walk on without the guidance of individual consciousness.

Reason itself is negated, the traditional quality that separates man from the rest of nature. "Kill the brain," the television announcers advise, "and you kill the ghoul." The head becomes the primary target of violence in the film — for your own protection, kill the brain! Richard McGuinness comes closest to realizing the full implications of the film when he describes the acting in it: "The actors' frenzies (of panicked flailing running, arduous pushing, fiendish clutching) are of an enthusiasm rarely seen in films but here look simply like reasonable responses to the circumstances." This frenzy does come to be the only reasonable act in the film, and at the end, with all brains killed among the central characters, only violence and the fire remain.

"It's not like just a wind that's passing through," Tom tells Judy before they go out to the truck. "We've got to do something fast." It isn't just a wind that's passing through; it is the ordinary world revealed for what it dangerously is. And the real horror of *Night of the Living Dead* is that there is nothing we can do that will make any difference at all. Whether that horror is the result of a cynicism with an eye to commercial gain, or (as Joseph Lewis suggests) a deliberate put-on, or a genuine nihilistic vision, its depth and the thoroughness of its unrelenting expression make the film what it is. It is in the bad, Wallace Stevens suggested, that "we reach/ The last purity of the good." *Night of the Living Dead* presents the bad with great force, but what good we reach in it is small and frail indeed.

SATYRICON:
"IF WE WERE ALL DEVILS . . ."

If *Night of the Living Dead* is a film which gains its power by the negation of human values and the emasculation of belief, Fellini's *Satyricon* would at first glance seem to be its twin. Exotic where Romero's film is ordinary, garishly colorful rather than dully black and white, fragmented structurally instead of organically unified, *Satyricon* does, however, lay open human failure with an intensity that asserts its kinship with *Night of the Living Dead* despite those differences. But, of course, Fellini's film, for all its immediate similiarity to Romero's nihilistic "symphony," does and is a great deal more than similarity might suggest.

According to Bernardino Zapponi, co-author of the screenplay of *Satyricon*, the film is "a psychedelic movie, historical science-fiction, a journey into time, a planetary world, away from our everyday logic and rhythm." Fellini has described it as "a 'science fiction' in the sense that it is a journey into the unknown — a planet like Mercury or Mars, but in this case a pagan planet." And certainly it is. The film shatters all of our normal ways of seeing and understanding; it thrusts us into a world so alien that, at first, we do not have any of the right concepts necessary to perceive what is happening before our eyes. John Simon, for example, found

Satyricon to be a series of "undigested dreams, the raw material of the subconscious, [that] do not make telling works of art." He could not make the film into the narrative whole that we have come to expect a movie (or any work of art) to be. But his expectations and the failure of the fulfillment of those expectations is part of the meaning of *Satyricon*. The film is fragmented precisely so that we will see and feel that fragmentation and know it for what it is. And by that knowing, we may come to an understanding of ourselves and of the world in which we live far richer than that which a less radical artistic form could have given us. By seeing the fragmentation of Fellini's alien world, we come to know both the dangers of fragmentation in and the wholeness of our own world with a fullness which most modern art and modern thought

In **Satyricon** Fortunata, her hair stacked up and back in an inverted pyramid, is a gaudy parody of a Roman matron.

has denied us. Fellini's *Satyricon* works on us by reversals, or as Zapponi would have it, "counterimages, counterdialogue."

But all of this is very abstract, a set of assertions. If the film is examined with some care, however, I believe that those assertions will hold true and that we will be able to see Fellini's *Satyricon* as a Christian *comedie noire*, a rendering in terror of the awful truth of life which enables us to "walk as children of the light."

There are as many possible approaches to a film of this complexity as there are images in it, but we must begin somewhere, and I propose to start with the figure of Fortunata, the wealthy "poet" Trimalchio's wife. She struck me as a familiar figure the first time she appeared, her hair stacked up and back in an inverted pyramid, a gaudy parody of a Roman matron. But I only recognized her when she and Scintilla pecked away at each other's

Fortunata is an echo of Elsa Lanchester as the monster's bride in **Bride of Frankenstein.**

lips, "like lizards, like doves." Then her awkwardness in the dance and all of her quick, birdlike motions came together to form an echo, an allusion to the image of Elsa Lanchester as the intended bride of the monster in Whale's *Bride of Frankenstein*. And the allusion is an appropriate one, for Fortunata is as alien to us as Doctor Frankenstein's second creature with her body sewn together from those of dead women and with a synthetic brain, a child of murder and mad science. Both move like lizards and birds, both are parodies of women, and both are beyond any rational analysis. Think of Fortunata's image, spattered with sauce thrown in her face by her husband, dancing grotesquely and gracelessly, she is, as Doctor Pretorius describes Frankenstein's initial creature, "a monstrous lampoon of the living."

Fortunata dances grotesquely and gracelessly, "a monstrous lampoon of the living."

From this likeness, we can go on to understand *Satyricon* as a horror film, more kin to Whale's *Frankenstein* and *Bride of Frankenstein* than to Mervyn LeRoy's *Quo Vadis* or Anthony Mann's *The Fall of the Roman Empire*. The traditional historical film has approached the Romans as if they were modern men in costume; the approach has been rational, and the resulting films have had the formal wholeness which John Simon could not find in Fellini's film. But Fellini, knowing that "Our vision of the Roman world has been distorted by textbooks," set out to imagine a world so alien that it could as well be inhabited by "Martians." His Romans do not inhabit a world that is "archeological, or historical, or nostalgic." They inhabit a world without Christ, the Land of Unlikeness without the possibility of the values inherent in salvation, a pagan and fallen world not reconstructed rationally by a modern thinker but imagined by a modern Christian artist, a world which is "a species of nebula . . . nourished by nothing."

But if the film is, as Fellini says, "a fantasy," can it also be science fiction or even Zapponi's "historical science-fiction"? If we accept the usual understanding of the nature of science fiction, I think not, for science fiction is concerned more with rational rather than imaginative extrapolation from fact, and it fails most often from a lack of imaginative vision. A character in Fred Hoyle's novel, *October the First Is Too Late*, states clearly the limitation of science fiction which is most appropriate to this discussion:

> *Science-fiction is a medium that concerns, above all else, life forms other than ourselves. The real life forms of our own planet belong of course to natural history, to zoology, so science-fiction purports to deal with life forms of the imagination. Yet what do we find when we read science-fiction? Nothing really but human beings. The brains of a creature of science-fiction are essentially human. You put such a brain inside a big lizard, and bangwallop, you have a science-fiction story.*

Fellini has gone much further toward creating "life forms of the imagination" than have Hoyle's science-fiction writers, for his human characters seem to have the brains of lizards or, even more accurately, synthetic brains like that of the bride of Frankenstein, brains thinking thoughts so alien to ours that we cannot understand or even see anything beyond the most superficial of resemblances.

But Fellini's *Satyricon* is more than a fulfillment of science fiction's possibilities, for its purposes are much closer to that of the horror film. The horror film, for all its concern with "life forms other than ourselves," is really concerned only with ourselves and with an accommodation of ourselves with the mysterious and awful world of sin and death in which we live. It is, in its classic form, primarily concerned with making us feel the mystery and wonder of life and with making us accept death as the natural ending of life, an ending to be desired. When Frankenstein's monster realizes in *Bride of Frankenstein* that he and his bride and the evil Doctor Pretorius all "belong dead," he is merely restating his creator's earlier fear that "Perhaps death is sacred, and I've profaned it." But if death is sacred, then life is sacred, too, and a film that accommodates us to the thought and the fact of death is also affirming the value of life with all of its perplexities and suffering.

When Fellini shows us pagans living without hope or meaning in a world, as he put it, "before Christ, before the invention of the conscience, of guilt," he is showing us the value of life as we know it by giving us a vision of the world without guilt and conscience, and without love which is the source of them both. If the sight of immortal creatures in horror films — vampires, werewolves, and Frankenstein's monsters — accommodate us by awful example to our mortality, then Fellini's guiltless pagans offer us a similar awful example which should accommodate us to ourselves and all of the necessary pain of a life of guilt and conscience and love. It is as if Fellini's *Satyricon* were an answer to a remark of Doctor Pretorius in *Bride of Frankenstein* when he says to Henry Frankenstein, "Sometimes I wonder if life wouldn't be much more amusing if we were all devils — with no nonsense about being angels and about being good." Perhaps Doctor Pretorius would find the nightmare world of *Satyricon* amusing, but it is just as deadly as the world of his own grotesque imaginings, a world of murder and death and a laughter that is only of the grave.

The world in which "we were all devils" is Fellini's ancient Rome, the land of his ancestors and of Italian glory, as alien to him as it is to us. It is the land of the living dead, people who are physically alive but spiritually dead, people who "belong dead" but do not have the Frankenstein monster's insight and self-knowledge. Trimalchio, the richest man in the film's world, the successful poet, is a figure from a horror film, one of the living dead. Fellini describes him as "a sort of gloomy, stolid Onassis, with a glazed look in his eye: a mummy," and he wanted Boris Karloff, the original mummy in Karl Freund's *The Mummy*, to take the part. He also wanted Licha, the grotesque, one-eyed imperial emissary to be played by "a Christopher Lee type." And how appropriate

The land is of the living dead with people who are physically alive but spiritually dead.

it would have been to have had two of Frankenstein's monsters in this grandest and most perfect of horror films.

There is no need to attempt a catalogue of the Roman horrors in the film; they fill it to overflowing. Fellini wishes the audience to "have the sensation of being surrounded by mysterious masks, ghosts and shadows the likes of which they have never seen before." The atmosphere of most of the first half of the film is itself horrible: the air is smoky or steamy, lit only by firelight and that often reflected from water; everything is dirty and dim; the elements themselves have no integrity, and fire, water, air and earth mingle obscenely in plastic confusion. Just before the collapse of the Insula Felices, the vast beehive building where Encolpius and Ascyltus live, Encolpius looks up and sees, far above, the night sky and its cold stars ("lidless stars" like those which look down on the "stricken" world at the end of Faulkner's "Dry September"). They are the same changeless stars he sees much later through the roof of the villa of the suicides. His world bursts and falls away beneath his feet or goes up in flames, but the stars remain overhead, distant and immutable, an indication of a larger harmony and wholeness that he seldom sees and never attempts to comprehend. His world is unstable, fragmented and pointless — a world without belief or meaning. The horror is completed by the presence of the stars. Even the monster in *Frankenstein* yearns for the light that flows down to him through the skylight and stretches his arms vainly to hold it, but Encolpius merely looks up at the sky, and we never know whether he really sees it or not.

If the world is unstable and disordered in *Satyricon*, human life is even more so. The film opens with Encolpius' lament for the loss of his slave, Giton. He speaks of himself as in exile, having escaped being swallowed by the earth and the sea, "left out in the cold, alone" by his friend Ascyltus who has stolen away Giton:

> *I loved you, Giton, I love you still . . . I can't share you with the others, because you are part of me, you are myself, you are my soul, and my soul belongs to me. You're the sun, you're the sea, you're all the gods at*

Encolpius and Giton, a perverse expression of love.

*once. I must find you, no matter what, or I am no longer
a man.*

From this perverse expression of love, totally erotic and distorting
Encolpius' perception of his world, the film moves on through a
world without real love, a world of cruelty and excess. The theatre
where Encolpius finds Giton offers us a first glimpse of the larger
world it mimes. It is a theatre of gross humor and cruelty. The
music is percussive; the clown Vernacchio plays a flat tune of farts.
Vernacchio is assisted by an assortment of grotesques, and the
center of his act is a "miracle" to be performed by divine Caesar.
A man's hand is lopped off on stage, but when Caesar commands
it, the hand is restored. But the new hand is of bronze, hastily tied

Vernacchio and Caesar's "miracle," with the "cured" man in shock, his jaws chattering while his blood drains.

on with scarves offstage, and the "cured" man is in shock, his jaws chattering while his blood drains. And for all this, the audience is bored; they are as grotesque themselves as anything on the stage. Justice intervenes when Encolpius demands the return of Giton. A magistrate forces Vernacchio to return the boy, but only because Vernacchio's "conduct has become unbearable" and his "arrogance is becoming tiresome." The world seen in small on Vernacchio's stage is cold and humorless despite all the jokes; its violence is cruel and pointless, and its justice is whimsical at best.

When Encolpius leaves with Giton, he simply enters the larger world which is no different from the smaller. There are no distinctions between art and reality in this world, none between fantasy and fact, because there is no "reality." The world is animal, each moment as real as each other, dream and reality both unreal, a world without a past and with no future. The past has been forgotten and its values corrupted; the future will simply be the same as the present. Throughout the film, poetry seems to represent the highest striving and achievement of the ancient world. But in Trimalchio's act, a poet is worse than a thief, a murderer, a raper and ravisher, and a pimp. Trimalchio, the successful poet, either writes doggerel or steals from Lucretius, and Eumolpus, who reveres the

Ariadne and the headless statue with nothing of what we think of as classical beauty.

great poetry of the past and is a real poet himself, is at one point almost thrown into Trimalchio's cooking fires like a hog "and the old man screams like a flayed cat." There are moments of beauty in the film, echoes of that classical beauty which our Renaissance forebears taught us to revere, but they are few and scattered, and they have no real potency in their surroundings of corruption. Even one of the statues in the art gallery where Encolpius meets Eumolpus has its head bandaged.

And the film moves on and on, to the street of whores, filled with grotesquerie and perversion, to Trimalchio's banquet where even the laughter seems organized and mirthless, to Trimalchio's tomb where a parody of death, grief and resurrection unfolds, to the ship of Licha, the villa of suicides, the hermaphrodite's cave, the labyrinth of the magic city, the garden of delights, Oenothea's house, the murder of Ascyltus, and finally to the death of Eumolpus by the sea. Everywhere the world constantly reverses itself. The manly and brutal Licha becomes Encolpius' simpering bride. The young Caesar is slain, and a new political order arises no different from the one before. Giton disappears and Encolpius does not seem even to remember him. The only calm, loving and traditionally "classical" man and woman in the film send their children away and commit suicide. Apparent dangers (the minotaur in the labyrinth) turn out to be jokes, and apparently innocent pleasures (Trimalchio's banquet) prove to be deadly serious. The world is turned upside down and inside out.

The people themselves seem scarcely human. Fortunata moves like a bird or a lizard, and throughout the film people exhibit characteristics of other animals. The inhabitants of the Insula Felices cry out "like the buzzing of maddened bees." Characters scuttle around like insects and rats. The boatman who kills Ascyltus looks like a fish. The film is peopled by dwarves and hunchbacks and huge fat men and women, so large as almost to be inhuman. And people speak in unknown tongues and with indecipherable gestures. The beautiful oriental slave girl at the villa of the suicides speaks a musical and primitive language, and she moves "like a cat." Giton moves his hands in a curious semaphore that we cannot interpret. These are all people who, in Fellini's words, are "so

The manly and brutal Licha becomes Encolpius' simpering bride.

distant from us, who eat and drink different things, who love in other ways, who have different habits, thoughts, even different nervous systems." But always they are recognizably human; they are our ancestors as well as Fellini's. And there is the horror.

The atmosphere and the corruption and the animal actions add up to a human world, one closer to the animal than ours, a world without hope, but a human world. And the absence of love,

The beautiful oriental slave girl at the villa of suicides.

of simple human caring beyond the erotic, makes that love as tangible and real as any work of art ever has. By our response to the horror, we find the knowledge of good in ourselves. We cannot identify with the central characters of *Satyricon* any more than we can with Count Dracula or the bride of Frankenstein, but we can see enough of ourselves in those characters to discover what we are that they are not. By the distancing of art, we come closer to what we are and what we value.

As in *Night of the Living Dead*, in the midst of the horrors, the "bad," we do find moments of genuine good, of unselfish love. Those moments here, too, are small and impotent. The kindly patrician who frees his slaves and loves his family dies by his own hand. The lovely oriental slave is alone and sad; when the two young men are asleep after their orgy, she "sings, pensive, absorbed, almost with tears in her eyes." Eumolpus offers Encolpius the melancholic gift of poetry, which is as well the gift of the natural world:

> I'll leave you my poetry. . . . I leave you life itself. I leave you the seasons, especially spring and summer. I leave you the wind, and the sun. I leave you the sea. The sea is good, and the earth, too, is good. I leave you the color of ripe grain; and the torrents and streams; the great clouds which fly solemnly and light . . . you'll look at them and perhaps you'll remember our brief friendship. And I leave you the trees and their busy inhabitants. Love, tears, happiness. The stars, Encolpius, I leave you those, too. I leave you sounds, songs, noises: the voice of man, which is the most harmonious of music . . . I leave you . . .

But Encolpius, drunk and full of Trimalchio's wine and food, is asleep. In the midst of a nightmare landscape, lit as if by the fires of hell, Encolpius sleeps and does not receive the gift of love and poetry, the gift of the world and the stars, not even the gift of self implied by the last fragmentary sentence.

There is one tale at the center of the larger tale which does contain a victory of love and life. It is the story of the Widow of Ephesus which a male prostitute tells in Trimalchio's tomb after the hideous parody of Trimalchio's burial has been enacted. The story transcends the circumstances of its telling and becomes a beautiful fable of life in the very face of death. In the story, the Widow remains in the tomb of her husband after the funeral party has departed. A young soldier, detailed to guard the corpse of a thief, hears her sobs and enters the tomb. "Don't you want to come back to life?" he asks her as he offers her food. They make love in the tomb, but when the soldier returns to his post, the thief's relatives have stolen his body away. The soldier returns to the tomb and offers to kill himself in his fear and despair, but the Widow stops him, saying, "No, my dear. To lose the two men in my life, one after the other, would be too much." She suggests that they substitute the corpse of her husband for the missing thief, and she adds, "I'd rather hang a dead husband than lose a living lover!"

The tale is a simple one, and Fellini presents it simply. The Widow's face is pale and deathly when she is mourning. After the lovemaking, it is warm and freshly colored. The body of the hushand is as dry and stiff as a matchstick as they carry it out. The lesson is simple and clear. The physical self is nothing without life, and life is nothing without love. Christ commanded that we "let the dead bury their dead," and the Widow of Ephesus knows that truth in her heart without ever hearing it. She acts out of her love, and her story is a true comedy in the center of a black comedy of grotesques.

If we are able to read the story of the Widow of Ephesus as a prefiguring of Christian truth, we have found another way of seeing Fellini's *Satyricon*, a way of understanding how it is different from *Night of the Living Dead*. The Widow's story shifts the emphasis of her understanding away from death to the living present and the possibilities of the future, precisely as Christ brings the life of the spirit back into the stricken world after the fall. Fellini's film is, although he says that its subject is "the pagan attitude to life before the coming of the Christian conscience," a web of Christian symbols, none of them quite clear or complete. It is as if the world were moving toward Christ, shaping itself to His coming. Think of these symbols, only a few of those in the film: the miracle of Caesar in Trimalchio's theatre which prefigures those of Christ, the white horse of death in the falling Insula Felices, the "resurrection" of Trimalchio in his tomb, the story of the Widow of Ephesus, Licha's ship which is shaped like a cross, Licha's appearing once like a Judas by Masaccio, the huge misshapen fish, the hermaphrodite visited by sheep and the crippled shepherds and attended by men who are dressed almost like modern priests, Oenothea's giving back fire to the world through her loins, Eumol-

The "resurrection" of Trimalchio in his tomb.

pus' forcing of those who would inherit his wealth to eat of his flesh, the uses throughout of fire and water. All of these are grotesque distortions of Christian emblems, just as the hideous wading bird in the house of Oenothea might be seen as a version of a stork (symbolic of the Annunciation) or of the pelican (which was thought to feed its young with its own blood, and therefore symbolizes Christ's sacrifice on the cross).

But none of the prefigurings is whole or undistorted, and none of the characters in the film can see any of these symbols forming, just as they cannot see the coming of Christ or even the spiritual nature of being. They are trapped in the flesh without spirit; they are forever in the darkness of pagan understanding.

Alberto Moravia stated part of Fellini's vision of the pagan world in its hellish aspects in an interview with Fellini in 1969:

> *All these monsters, whether hideous or beautiful, that you've crammed into your film, all these albino hermaphrodites, these hairy dwarfs, these elephantine prostitutes, these lascivious Gitons, these paralytic, maimed, dropsical, truncated, blind, halt, and lame etcetera people, reveal, besides your own baroque temperament with its inclination to wildly unrestrained imagination, the idea that antiquity signified nature without soul, sunk in the depths of irremediable corruption. . . . In fact the monster exemplifies corruption not of the spirit but of the body; not moral, but physical, putrefaction. Antiquity for you is nature once limpid, pure and young, then degenerate and fallen into decay. It is no mere chance that the dark, subterranean, sordid, mysterious surroundings of your film suggest the idea of the Inferno. An inferno that is in no wise moral but wholly physical, like that of certain primitive painters before Dante. An inferno without purgatory and without paradise.*

Moravia sees that Fellini's pagan Rome is an inferno, but he overlooks the prefigurings of Christ's coming throughout the film. Moravia accuses Fellini of seeing the pagan world like an early and primitive Christian, and certainly Eumolpus' value in the film does seem to rest in his anticipating Christian truths without the aid of Revelation. But Fellini is no medieval Christian; he is simply a Christian, unorthodox and often anti-clerical, but a Christian, shaping his artistic and moral perception to Christian belief and making his fictive worlds to conform to the truth of his Christian vision.

Fellini has always been a Christian artist, as his European critics have usually seen when his American critics have not. *La Dolce Vita* is an "Inferno," and *8½* is as much a "Purgatorio." The love at the heart of *Juliet of the Spirits* (*Giulietta degli Spiriti*), like that of *I Clowns* and *Amarcord*, may in fact render it more a "Paradiso" than is at first apparent. And *Satyricon* has deep roots in Fellini's belief and strong bonds to his other work. Like *La Dolce Vita* it is an "Inferno," sharing with that film the image of a monstrous fish which appears to the meandering central characters of both films as an emblem of earthly corruption rather than Christian hope. Perhaps Paola's smile at the end of *La Dolce Vita* and the sunrise at the end of *Satyricon* indicate the future of love and hope that is available to those who have eyes to see, to the viewer of the films, even if the central characters in those films can only walk or sail away into hopelessness.

There is an ambiguity in the ending of *Satyricon* which is intriguing and appropriate to the film. In the treatment, the film was to have ended with a scene in which the Roman gods appear to Encolpius but are dispersed back into nature "Whence they sprung" by the rising sun. Encolpius, like Marcello, "walks on," godless and without even the illusion of soul. But in the film itself, Encolpius rejects the dead flesh of Eumolpus and sails away with the crew of young men. He tells us that "On an island covered by high sweet-scented grasses a young Greek introduced himself and told me that in the year. . . ." But he does not go on; the colors of the sea fade away, and we are left only with a broken wall on which the faces of the characters in the film appear in an ancient fresco, all of them "with ambiguous smiles." Perhaps the young Greek told Encolpius the truth of Christ, but we cannot know. A pagan book, even when translated into film by a Christian artist, must remain forever short of the truth. Like Virgil in Dante's *Divine Comedy*, Petronius may take us only to the gates of Paradise, but he may never enter. The Christian vision of the film is Fellini's and we may share it with grace and joy, but the world of pagan Rome must remain true to Petronius, a fragmented world which can be made whole only by later Christian understanding.

Satyricon is finally a film about seeing. Think of the eyes which are appropriate to its texture: Licha's glass eye, Trimalchio's eyes in the wall mozaic, Oenothea's startling blue eyes. One of the earliest images in the film is of a giant stone head being drawn by horses down a narrow Roman street, its eyes dominating the

*The Romans were as blind and alien as statues or paintings
to our way of seeing and understanding.*

screen, open, empty, forever blind. None of the characters in the
film is able to escape that blindness. How appropriate that we
know the Romans by their statues, for, as we learn in the film, they
were as blind and as alien as statues to our way of seeing and
understanding. And our rational, intellectual understanding of the
Romans is just as blind (we should always remember the suicide
of the intellectual Steiner in *La Dolce Vita*, for his dependence
on reason is as futile as the pagans' spiritual blindness in *Satyricon*).
But Fellini gives us a visual understanding of that alien world
which transcends fragmentation and blindness. By an art of light
and motion, he gives us the opportunity to see the growing truth

of the world through the empty motions of his alien and pagan characters.

W. R. Robinson's statement of the power of the cinema as an art of light is especially appropriate to an understanding of *Satyricon:*

> *In a world of light and a light world — unanalyzable, uninterpretable, without substance or essence, meaning or direction — being and non-being magically breed existence. Out of the darkness and chaos of the theater beams a light; out of the nothingness is generated brilliant form, existence suspended somewhere between the extremes of total darkness and total light. Performing its rhythmic dance to energy's tune, the movie of the imagination proves, should there be any doubt, that cinema, an art of light, contributes more than any other art today to fleshing out the possibilities for good within an imaginative universe.*

Fellini's images formed in light give us a living Roman world in full color, but the colors are hot and garish and the living world is without spirit, a world of the living dead. And these imaginary characters — imagined by Petronius, reimagined by Fellini, reimagined by each of us in creative communion with them both — all are dead at the end of the film, are all figures on a crumbling wall. The film is a Christian horror film, but it is also a parable of art much like *8½*. None of the characters of the narrative are alive; they are all unreal, all dead, but by caring and by imagining we give them life, and the truth of their borrowed lives stays alive in us and in our lives after they have returned to the death and unreality of the painted wall, the closed book, the dark room and the reel of film in the can. So, Fellini would have us know, do we all live by the grace of God, and we shall continue to live by the love of Christ which is the love of God. By seeing, we know; by imagining, we love; by knowing and loving, we live.

I have not even begun to exhaust the possibilities for learning available to us in Fellini's *Satyricon*, for, as in the chapter on *Frankenstein*, I have mentioned only a few approaches to the film among very, very many. I could have discussed Fellini's use of color in the film: how its brightness and garishness contrasts to the muted and harmonious colors in Antonioni's humanistic *Red Desert (Il deserto rosso)* or *Blow Up*, or Fellini's own *Amarcord*, or how the tone of the colors change as the film progresses toward the coming of Christ and the natural light of the dawn (only to slip back to the bright, false colors of the broken pagan wall at the very end). Or, I could have discussed Fellini's fidelity to Petronius. The possibilities, as I said, are very many. But I shall conclude by returning directly to the idea of *Satyricon* as a horror film.

Since the decline of the horror film as a pure form after the great films of the 1930s and 1940s, there have been few genuinely fine horror films. Hitchcock's *Psycho* and Polanski's *Repulsion* come to mind, but they are both closer to psychological realism than they are to parabolic films like Dreyer's *Vampyr*, Whale's two Frankenstein pictures, *The Wolf Man*, Tod Browning's *Freaks*, Karl Freund's *Mad Love*, or Edgar G. Ulmer's *The Black Cat*. One of the difficulties, I suspect, is the advent of color. The great horror films were fashioned of black and white, just as their moral structure juxtaposed within them good and evil, life and death. When the English filmmakers at Hammer and other studios attempted to re-make the black and white films in color, they succeeded in making some handsome films, but few in which color was able to function as a meaningful part of the parable. To my mind, they failed, although David Pirie does make strong arguments to the contrary in *A Heritage of Horror*. Roger Corman's films are so lushly color-ful that no one could take even their nights and shadows seriously, so they have appropriately been transformed into comedies. *The Exorcist* and its occult imitators share that lushness and that failure. The richness of Vadim's *Blood and Roses (Et Mourir de Plaisir)* and Nicolas Roeg's *Don't Look Now* is appropriate to their air of decadence, and Roman Polanski used the color in *The Fearless Vampire Killers (Dance of the Vampires)* and *Rosemary's Baby* brilliantly as did Ken Russell in *The Devils*, but for the most part color has hindered more than helped the job of creating artistically valid horror films. Fellini's *Satyricon* is the brilliant exception; it is a film that cannot be conceived of in black and white. It has the parabolic richness of the earlier horror films, because Fellini was able to use color with the same skill with which Whale used black and white.

Aside from the problem of color, another reason the horror film has lost validity as a pure form is that postwar existential thought has questioned the validity of metaphor and parable in all art forms. The present high esteem, however, with which Nabokov and Borges and García Márquez are held is evidence that existential realism is burning itself out in fiction, and the success of filmmakers like Bergman and Fellini, Russell and Roeg, is evidence that the same thing is happening in serious films. Both Bergman and Fellini have been Christian filmmakers all along. Despite the darkness which is often such an important part of their vision, both of them have questioned the existential despair which has been fragmenting our understanding and draining our creative vitality. Bergman returned directly to the medieval vision in films like *The Seventh Seal (Det Sjunde Inseglet)* and *The Virgin Spring (Jungfrukällen)* from which he gained a sense of wholeness and a strength of belief which enabled him to make his later trilogy and films like *Persona* which test directly the lack of center and fragmentation of modern despair. And Fellini's *8½*, *Juliet of the Spirits* and *Amarcord* are fulfillments of his ambition "to restore fantasy to the cinema" and are certainly testaments to his faith in the ability of the imagination to create a whole out of the shards and orts of contemporary disbelief.

It is only natural, then, for these two filmmakers to have made the finest horror films since the thirties — Bergman's *Hour of the Wolf* and Fellini's *Satyricon*, both of which are not formally pure horror films, but both of which allude directly to the horror films of the thirties and both of which strive for that fantasy which is no substitute for reality but which is able to make reality truer and somehow more real by renewing the clarity of our perception. At least by seeing them as horror films, we are able to see both those richly enigmatic and perplexing films with a beginning of proper understanding.

At the Film Institute in Hollywood in early 1969, Fellini said that "My *Satyricon* is even more autobiographical than my *8½*," and *Satyricon* is autobiographical in the way *Hour of the Wolf* is, or *Bride of Frankenstein*. Made almost entirely in the controlled world of the studio, it imaginatively recounts a portion of the auto-biography of the inner life, of the life of the spirit, a life which we all share and know. It is autobiographical, but it is impersonal, in the way that C. Day Lewis said that a lyric poem is impersonal, "not because the poet has deliberately screened personal feelings or memories out of it, but because he has broken *through them* to the ground of their being, a ground which is the fruitful compost made by the numberless human experiences of like nature." Fellini said, after the completion of *Satyricon*, that it destroyed the need in him "to identify myself sentimentally and ideologically with the subject," and that he had made the film with "complete detach-ment." That detachment comes from his having "broken through" to the ground of our shared being, beyond the personal, the senti-mental and the ideological to the true.

At the end of his preface to the treatment of the film, Fellini says that he wished to embody "the eternal myth; man standing alone before the fascinating mystery of life, all its terror, its beauty and its passion." To my mind, he has done just that and a great deal more, for you are not alone in the darkness and chaos of the movie theater in which you see *Satyricon*. You are actually creating a world in imaginative communion with Federico Fellini, a world mysterious, terrifying, beautiful, and passionate. And that world of your imagining, alien and awful as it may be, opens to you, be-cause of that communal act of imagination, the mystery and beauty of the living world, our own.

THE CIRCLE DRAWN

The values which *Frankenstein* offers its viewers may be roughly divided into four general categories. First, the film gives us a sense of the positive value of striving for perceptual and moral growth. Henry Frankenstein yearns for the answers to the largest of all questions and for the great ray, the light beyond seeing. His yearning expresses itself in his use of the great ray in the world for the creation of a living being, one capable of understanding and of free moral action. His creation, too, yearns for the light, and he grows in the film toward a fulfillment of the potential that Henry intended for him. The evil in the film is not unleashed by either Henry or his monster's reaching out. It is rather the result of Henry's failure to see the presence of shadow as well as light in the living world and his failure to follow his actions through to their proper end. His surrender of the moral responsibility for correcting the results of his own perceptual failure leads directly to the monster's crimes and to the failure of both their strivings in destructive fire.

The sympathy which the film rouses in the viewer for both Henry and the monster is the film's second major value. This sympathy heals the breach between creator and created and allows the

Frankenstein *rouses sympathy in the
viewer for both Henry and the monster.*

viewer to experience fully both the largeness of their striving and the hurt of their failure. That sympathy also renders the film's third major value, an understanding of the reasons for that failure, experientially operative. The viewer understands Henry's moral failure and its reflection in the behavior of his monster, but the real sympathy for them both does not allow him to deny the value of their striving by a harsh judgment of its failure. Rather it enlarges the viewer's perception and allows him to feel the rightness of the film's ending in the light and of the closed door which severs Henry and Elizabeth from the narrow and closed world of the Baron and the past. In other words, the active esthetic cooperation of sympathy and understanding in the film lead directly to its open end, its sense of ongoing possibility.

And finally, the conscious artificiality of the sets, the expansiveness of the acting, the elaborately controlled function of literal light and shadow in the film's narrative design, all of these support the thematic movement toward continuing possibility by drawing a circle one step larger than that of literal and ordinary direct "reality." The whole film expresses the human consciousness' need for "enormous vistas" and its strength to overcome even the obstacles of its own failings to create and maintain those vistas. *Frankenstein* is no ecstatic hymn to human perfection, but it is an honest expression of the human's need to strive for growth and towards perfection, in response to the urging of the universe itself.

The Wolf Man lacks *Frankenstein's* cosmic largeness in theme and texture. The striving which it delineates is not for larger human growth, but for the maintenance of individual moral freedom and individual happiness. The book, the given circle, is tested in this film, but it maintains its supremacy; no circle is drawn beyond the one drawn by the definition of lycanthropy in the book of the opening shot. If the striving is diminished, the sympathy of the viewer is diminished as well. It is closer to pity than to identification, and its conclusion is closer to sadness than to the annealed awareness of *Frankenstein*.

That diminished sympathy still leads the viewer to an understanding of the failure of Lawrence Talbot's striving, but the source of Larry's failure — his inability to use both head and hand together

*In **The Wolf Man**, Larry is a victim, caught
by his own biological nature.*

— seems to be simply a part of his biological nature, beyond cor-
rection. When Larry's mental confusion causes him to miss the
wolf in the shooting gallery, it is an emblematic confession of the
nature of his failure, and its only explanation would seem to be
Maleva's in the following scene — that he is a victim, that the way
he walks is thorny literally through no fault of his own. The lack
of freedom in Larry's struggle, its fatalistic quality, renders the
film's ending appropriate to that struggle, but it denies it the opportunity of expressing, or even implying, further possibility. The film's
darkening, its loss of light, is the proper textural expression of
Larry's struggle, but its restricting of Larry's freedom and its closed
end seem to deny, as I have said, the primary qualities of its forward motion.

The Wolf Man is, then, a smaller film than *Frankenstein,* thematically and texturally. Its response is less forceful and rewarding to the demands of its cultural context. It still emphasizes the necessity for moral struggle, and it rouses a genuine sympathy for that struggle, but it denies its final validity and disallows the possibilities of human growth.

Night of the Living Dead carries this devolution of values much further than *The Wolf Man.* The striving in the film, although still involved with the maintenance of individual identity, is primarily one for minimal survival. Where Lawrence Talbot regained at least his human form and a moral victory in self-destruction,

In **Night of the Living Dead,** the characters become food, or walking dead flesh, or simply fuel for a fire.

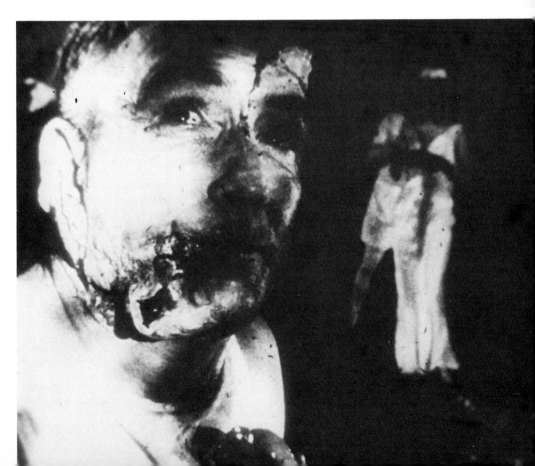

the characters in *Night of the Living Dead* lose all identity — they become food, or walking dead flesh, or simply fuel for a fire. The considerable sympathy that is gained for them in the first half of the film is lost in the frenzied horrors of the second half and finally burned on Ben's funeral pyre. No understanding of their failure to survive is offered as an anodyne for that painful loss of sympathy except the equally painful answer of accident and chance; their striving failed because it failed and not because of what it was. And, of course, the ending of the film is not only closed, it denies even the central equation of life and motion. Life and motion are shattered into static fragments, and then motion itself is equated with death in the last image of the moving flames. The circle which *Night of the Living Dead* draws is not beyond the

A fragmented and absurd world is pictured in **Satyricon** in the context of a larger world of possibility, meaning and value.

circle with which the viewer enters the theatre (as in *Frankenstein*), nor is it a retracing of that same circle (as in *The Wolf Man*); it draws a new circle within and much smaller than that circle. Its moral progress is actually atavistic and anti-evolutionary.

Fellini's *Satyricon* creates a reduction of a different sort, one which pictures a fragmented and absurd world in the context of the larger world of possibility, meaning and value shared by director and viewer alike. The reduction of values in the imagined pagan world is the prelude to a renewal of understanding and appreciation in the film's viewers of their own potentiality and strength in a world redeemed by the Christian incarnation, or, if you prefer to put it in different terms, a world redeemed by the vital force of love and light. The circle drawn in *Satyricon* is, then, a moving circle, expanding like a round ripple of water moving away from the splash of a stone tossed into its center. It is at once smaller than the circle with which the viewer enters the theatre, then as he gains awareness through the cinematic experience the same, and finally larger in the way that *Frankenstein*'s is, suggesting the inherent possibility in human experience of moving beyond the fragmentation of a life limited by the flesh and its myriad corruptions to one in which flesh and spirit are joined in a vital harmony. The film's moral progress operates by reversals, as in Wallace Stevens' poem, revealing the good in its absence, wholeness in fragmentation, direction in apparently random motion.

Any response to and judgment of these films is, then, finally metaphysical. If a viewer chooses *Frankenstein* as an example of a valid and significant esthetic expression of experience, then he has chosen an understanding of the nature of life which is light-centered, progressive, open and ongoing — a life in which moral freedom is the natural human condition. If he chooses *The Wolf Man*, he has chosen a life which is fate-centered, static, closed and circular — a life in which moral limitation is the natural human condition. If he chooses *Night of the Living Dead*, he has chosen a life which is death centered, regressive, closed and closing in — a life in which moral failure is the natural human condition. If he chooses Fellini's *Satyricon*, he has chosen a life which is life-centered, moving, dangerous but opening out — a life in which moral striving is the natural human condition.

When Count Dracula bids you, in *Dracula*, to "Listen to them, children of the night," he is offering you a clear alternative to Christ's command (John 12:35-36) that you "Walk while ye have the light, lest darkness come upon you," and that "While ye have light, believe in the light, that ye may be children of the light." That moral and metaphysical choice is, of course, implicit in any serious work of art. These four films, each in its own way, offer that same choice. By the terms that I have suggested, the choice is a clear one, for a commitment to the enhancement of life and to a truthful use of the qualities of the medium demands of us a choice of energy, of free moral action and of light. As Joyce Cary indicated, the great virtue of a work of art is that only in it is the choice ever made so fully and so precisely clear, and for that reason these four horror films are of real and serious value to the individual moral consciousness. Once textural and structural analysis has revealed the precise nature of the terms of that choice in each of these films, the very clarity and seriousness of the choice explains, to my mind, the reason for engaging in such an analysis and the lasting quality and worth of these films.

When they have been treated by their makers as a serious work of art, horror films have always made the nature of that choice clear with parabolic intensity, using the dark force of nightmare to cleanse our perceptions of the day. The horror film may no longer exist as a pure genre, but its lessons and methods have entered the cinematic mainstream where they continue to operate on us with the same vital impact, bidding us choose with visceral intensity again and again whether we truly belong to death or life, to night or light.

FILMOGRAPHY

FRANKENSTEIN (1931)

Universal. Producer: Carl Laemmle, Jr. Director: James Whale. Script: Garrett Fort, Francis Edwards Farragoh with (uncredited) Robert Florey; based on the play by Peggy Webling and the novel by Mrs. Percy B. Shelley. Director of Photography: Arthur Edeson. Editor: Clarence Kolster.

Cast: Colin Clive (Henry Frankenstein), Mae Clarke (Elizabeth), John Boles (Victor Moritz), Boris Karloff (The Monster), Edward Van Sloan (Doctor Waldman), Frederick Kerr (Baron Frankenstein), Dwight Frye (Fritz), Lionel Belmore (The Burgomaster), Marilyn Harris (Little Maria).
Running time: 71 mins.

THE WOLF MAN (1941)

Universal. Producer: George Waggner. Director: George Waggner. Script: Curt Siodmak. Director of Photography: Joseph Valentine. Editor: Ted Kent. Music: Charles Previn.

Cast: Claude Rains (Sir John Talbot), Ralph Bellamy (Col. Paul Montford), Evelyn Ankers (Gwen Conliffe), Warren William (Dr. Lloyd), Patric Knowles (Frank Andrews), Bela Lugosi (Bela the Gypsy), Lon Chaney, Jr. (Lawrence Talbot), Maria Ouspenskaya (Maleva), Fay Helm (Jennie Williams).
Running time: 71 mins.

NIGHT OF THE LIVING DEAD (1968)

Continental (The Walter Reade Organization). Producer: Russell Streiner & Karl Hardman. Director: George A. Romero. Script: John Russo; based on an uncredited story by George A. Romero inspired by Richard Matheson's novel, *I Am Legend*. Director of Photography: George A. Romero. Editor: George A. Romero. Title Sequence: The Animators.

Cast: Duane Jones (Ben), Judith O'Dea (Barbara), Russell Streiner (Johnny), Karl Hardman (Harry Cooper), Keith Wayne (Tom), Judith Ridley (Judy), Marilyn Eastman (Helen Cooper), Kyra Schon (Karen Cooper), Bill Caudille (Newscaster), Frank Doak (Dr. Grimes).
Running time: 90 mins.

SATYRICON (1969)

United Artists. Producer: Alberto Grimaldi. Director: Federico Fellini. Script: Federico Fellini & Bernardino Zapponi; freely adapted from the book by Petronius Arbiter. Director of Photography: Giuseppe Rotunno. Editor: Ruggero Mastroianni. Music: Nino Rota & Ilhan Mimaroglu, Ted Dockstader and Andrew Rudin.

Cast: Martin Potter (Encolpius), Hiram Keller (Ascyltus), Max Born (Giton), Fanfulla (Vernacchio), Salvo Randone (Eumolpus), Il More (Mario Romagnoli) (Trimalchio), Magali Noel (Fortunata), Alain Cuny (Licha), Lucia Bose (The matron), Joseph Wheeler (The suicide), Hylette Adolphe (The slave girl), Tanya Lopert (The emperor), Donyale Luna (Oenothea).
Running time: 120 mins.

SELECTIVE BIBLIOGRAPHY

Although this bibliography is by no means complete, I have attempted to include as many of the important books on the horror film (or with material in them on the horror film) as possible. The collection of articles is less complete and more selective. I have omitted articles from the major magazines devoted exclusively to the genre except in a few instances when they relate especially to the films I have discussed at length in this book. The size of this bibliography itself offers testimony to the growing serious interest in the horror film, and I shall allow it to speak for itself without further comment. I do, however, wish to thank Elizabeth Wise who did much of the work in its preparation.

BOOKS

Ackerman, Forrest J. *The Best From Famous Monsters of Filmland.* New York: Paperback Library, 1964.
_____. *Famous Monsters of Filmland Strike Back.* New York: Paperback Library, 1965.
_____. *The Frankenscience Monster.* New York: Ace, 1969.

————. *Son of Famous Monsters of Filmland.* New York: Paper-back Library, 1965.

Agee, James. *Agee on Film.* New York: McDowell, Obolensky, 1958.

Amis, Kingsley. *What Became of Jane Austen? And Other Questions.* New York: Harcourt Brace Jovanovich, 1970.

Anobile, Richard J., ed. *Frankenstein.* New York: Avon, 1974.

————, ed. *Psycho.* New York: Avon, 1974.

Aylesworth, Thomas G. *Monsters From the Movies.* Philadelphia: Lippincott, 1972.

Barber, Dulan. *Monsters Who's Who.* New York: Crescent, 1974.

Baxter, John. *An Appalling Talent: Ken Russell.* London: Michael Joseph, 1973.

————. *Hollywood in the Thirties.* New York: A.S. Barnes, 1968.

————. *Science Fiction in the Cinema.* New York: A.S. Barnes, 1970.

————. *Sixty Years of Hollywood.* New York: A.S. Barnes, 1973.

————. *Stunt: The Story of the Great Movie Stuntmen.* Garden City: Doubleday, 1973.

Beck, Calvin Thomas. *Heroes of the Horrors.* New York: Macmillan, 1975.

Bessy, Maurice. *Orson Welles.* New York: Crown, 1971.

Bjorkman, Stig, Torsten Manns, and Jonas Sima. *Bergman on Bergman.* New York: Simon & Schuster, 1973.

Bogdanovich, Peter. *The Cinema of Alfred Hitchcock.* New York: Museum of Modern Art Film Library, 1963.

———— in collaboration with Orson Welles. *This Is Orson Welles.* New York: Harper & Row, 1972.

Bojarski, Richard, and Kenneth Beals. *The Films of Boris Karloff.* New York: Citadel, 1975.

Bauche, Freddy. *The Cinema of Luis Buñuel.* New York: A.S. Barnes, 1973.

Budgen, Suzanne. *Fellini.* London: British Film Institute, 1966.

Butler, Ivan. *The Cinema of Roman Polanski.* New York: A.S. Barnes, 1970.

————. *The Horror Film.* New York: A.S. Barnes, 1967.

————. *Horror in the Cinema.* New York: A.S. Barnes, 1970.

Clarens, Carlos. *An Illustrated History of the Horror Film*. New York: Putnam, 1967.

Cooper, John C. and Carl Skrade, eds. *Celluloid and Symbols*. Philadelphia: Fortress, 1970.

Copper, Basil. *The Vampire in Legend, Fact and Art*. New York: Citadel, 1974.

Cowie, Peter. *The Cinema of Orson Welles*. New York: A.S. Barnes, 1965.

_____. *A Ribbon of Dreams: The Cinema of Orson Welles*. New York: A.S. Barnes, 1973.

Crist, Judith. *The Private Eye, the Cowboy, and the Very Naked Girl*. New York: Holt, Rinehart and Winston, 1968.

Douglas, Drake (pseud.). *Horror!* New York: Macmillan, 1966.

Dreyer, Carl Theodor. *Four Screenplays*. Bloomington, Ind.: Indiana University Press, 1964.

Durgnat, Raymond. *Eros in the Cinema*. London: Calder & Boyars, 1966.

_____. *Franju*. Berkeley: University of California Press, 1967.

_____. *Luis Buñuel*. Berkeley: University of California Press, 1967.

_____. *The Strange Case of Alfred Hitchcock*. Boston: MIT Press, 1974.

Edelson, Edward. *Great Monsters of the Movies*. Garden City: Doubleday, 1973.

Eisner, Lotte. *The Haunted Screen*. Berkeley: University of California Press, 1969.

Everson, William K. *The Bad Guys: A Pictorial History of the Movie Villain*. New York: Citadel, 1964.

_____. *Classics of the Horror Film*. New York: Citadel, 1974.

Eyles, Allen, Robert Adkinson and Nichols Fry. *The House of Horror: The Story of Horror Films*. London: Lorrimer, 1973.

Farber, Manny. *Negative Space*. New York: Praeger, 1971.

Fellini, Federico. *Fellini's Satyricon*. Ed. by Dario Zanelli. New York: Ballantine, 1970.

Frank, Alan G. *Horror Movies: Tales of Terror in the Cinema*. London: Octopus, 1974.

Gibson, Arthur. *The Silence of God: Creative Response to the Films of Ingmar Bergman*. New York: Harper & Row, 1969.

Gifford, Denis. *Karloff: The Man, the Monster, the Movies.* New York: Curtis, 1973.

———. *Movie Monsters.* New York: Dutton, 1969.

———. *A Pictorial History of Horror Movies.* New York: Hamlyn, 1973.

Glut, Donald F. *The Frankenstein Legend: A Tribute to Mary Shelley and Boris Karloff.* Metuchen, N.J.: Scarecrow Press, 1973.

Gow, Gordon. *Suspense in the Cinema.* New York: A.S. Barnes, 1968.

Greene, Graham. *Graham Greene on Film: Collected Film Criticism, 1935-1939.* New York: Simon & Schuster, 1972.

Haining, Peter, ed. *The Ghouls.* With an introduction by Vincent Price and an afterword by Christopher Lee. New York: Stein & Day, 1971.

Higham, Charles. *The Films of Orson Welles.* Berkeley: University of California Press, 1970.

——— and Joel Greenberg, eds. *The Celluloid Muse: Hollywood Directors Speak.* Chicago: Regnery, 1969.

———. *Hollywood in the Forties.* New York: A.S. Barnes, 1968.

Huss, Roy and T. J. Ross, eds. *Focus on the Horror Film.* Englewood Cliffs, N.J.: Prentice Hall, 1972.

Hutchinson, Tom. *Horror & Fantasy in the Movies.* New York: Crescent, 1974.

Jensen, Paul M. *Boris Karloff and His Films.* New York: A.S. Barnes, 1974.

Knight, Arthur. *The Liveliest Art.* New York: New American Library, 1957.

Kracauer, Siegfried. *From Caligari to Hitler.* Princeton: Princeton University Press, 1947.

Kyrou, Ado. *Luis Buñuel.* New York: Simon & Schuster, 1963.

———. *Le Surréalisme au Cinéma.* Paris: Edition Arcanes, 1953.

Laclos, Michel. *La Fantastique au Cinéma.* Paris: Pauvert, 1958.

LaValley, Albert J., ed. *Focus on Hitchcock.* Englewood Cliffs, N.J.: Prentice Hall, 1972.

Lee, Walt. *Reference Guide to Fantastic Films: Science Fiction, Fantasy & Horror.* 3 vols. Los Angeles: Chelsea-Lee, 1972.

Lennig, Arthur. *The Count: The Life and Films of Bela "Dracula" Lugosi*. New York: Putnam, 1974.

Lindsay, Vachel. *The Art of the Moving Picture*. New York: Macmillan, 1922.

Manchel, Frank. *Terrors of the Screen*. Englewood Cliffs, N.J.: Prentice Hall, 1970.

Masters, Anthony. *The Natural History of the Vampire*. New York: Putnam, 1972.

McBride, Joseph. *Orson Welles*. New York: Viking, 1972.

Milne, Tom. *The Cinema of Carl Dreyer*. New York: A.S. Barnes, 1971.

————. *Mamoulian*. Bloomington, Ind.: Indiana University Press, 1969.

Moss, Robert F. *Karloff and Company: The Horror Film*. New York: Pyramid, 1974.

Perry, George. *The Films of Alfred Hitchcock*. New York: Dutton, 1965.

Pirie, David. *A Heritage of Horror: The English Gothic Cinema 1946-1972*. New York: Avon, 1973.

Rohmer, Eric and Claude Chabrol. *Hitchcock*. Paris: Editions Universitaires, 1957.

Rotha, Paul. *The Film Till Now*. London: Vision, 1949.

Russo, John. *Night of the Living Dead*. With a preface by George Romero. New York: Warner Paperback Library, 1974.

Salachas, Gilbert. *Federico Fellini*. New York: Crown, 1969.

Sarris, Andrew. *The American Cinema: Directors and Directions 1929-1968*. New York: Dutton, 1968.

Siegel, Joel E. *Val Lewton: The Reality of Terror*. New York: Viking, 1973.

Simon, John. *Ingmar Bergman Directs*. New York: Harcourt Brace Jovanovich, 1972.

Simsolo, Noel. *Alfred Hitchcock*. Paris: Editions Seghers, 1969.

Solmi, Angelo. *Fellini*. New York: Humanities Press, 1968.

Steiger, Brad. *Monsters, Maidens and Mayhem: A Pictorial History of Horror Film Monsters*. New York: Merit, 1965.

Steinbrunner, Chris and Burt Goldblatt. *Cinema of the Fantastic*. New York: Saturday Review Press, 1972.

Stephenson, Ralph and J.R. Debrix. *The Cinema as Art*. London: Penguin, 1965.

Taylor, John Russell. *Cinema Eye, Cinema Ear*. New York: Hill & Wang, 1964.

Truffaut, François. *Hitchcock*. New York: Simon & Schuster, 1967.

Underwood, Peter. *Karloff: The Life of Boris Karloff*. New York: Drake, 1972.

Weergaard, Ebbe. *Carl Dreyer*. London: British Film Institute, 1950.

Wiene, Robert. *The Cabinet of Doctor Caligari*. New York: Simon & Schuster, 1970.

Wood, Robin. *Hitchcock's Films*. New York: A.S. Barnes, 1965.

_____. *Ingmar Bergman*. New York: Praeger, 1969.

Young, Vernon. *Cinema Borealis: Ingmar Bergman and the Swedish Ethos*. New York: David Lewis, 1971.

Zinman, David. *Fifty Classic Motion Pictures: The Stuff That Dreams Are Made Of*. New York: Crown, 1970.

ARTICLES

Addams, Charles, "Movie Monster Rally," *New York Times Magazine* (August 9, 1953), 16-17.

Alloway, Lawrence, "Monster Films," *Encounter*, XIV (January, 1960), 70-72.

Alpert, Hollis, "Fellini at Work," *Saturday Review*, LII (July 12, 1969), 14-17.

Ashmore, Jerome, "*The Cabinet of Dr. Caligari* as Fine Art," *College Art Journal*, IX (Summer, 1950), 412-418.

Atkins, Thomas R., "*Dr. Jekyll and Mr. Hyde*: An Interview With Rouben Mamoulian," *The Film Journal*, II (January-March, 1973), 36-44.

Barr, Charles, and Peter van Bagh, "*Repulsion*," *Movie* (Autumn, 1965), 26-28.

Beck, Calvin T., "Night of the Living Dead," *Castle of Frankenstein* V, No. 2 (1972), 30.

Belz, Carl, "The Birds," *Film Culture* (Winter, 1963-64), 51-53.

Berch, B., "Gold in Them Chills," *Collier's*, CXIII (January 29, 1944), 66.

Block, Alex B., "Filming *Night of the Living Dead*: An Interview With Director George Romero," *Filmmakers Newsletter*, V (January, 1972), 19-24.

Bodeen, DeWitt, "Val Lewton," *Films in Review*, XIV (March, 1963), 210-225.

Bogdanovich, Peter, "On *The Birds*," *Film Culture* (Spring, 1963), 69-70.

Bradbury, Ray, "A New Ending to *Rosemary's Baby*," *Films and Filming* (August, 1969), 10.

Brakhage, Stan, "Carl Theodore Dreyer," *Caterpillar* (January, 1971), 58-72.

Brighton, Lew, "Saturn in Retrograde or The Texas Jump Cut," *The Film Journal*, II, No. 4 (1975), 24-27.

Brower, Brock, "The Vulgarization of American Demonology," *Esquire*, LXI (June, 1964), 94-99.

Brustein, Robert, "Film Chronicles: Reflections on Horror Movies," *Partisan Review*, XXV (Spring, 1958), 288-296.

Cameron, Ian, "Eyes Without a Face," *Film* (November-December, 1960), 22-25.

Cohen, John, "On Being a Teenage Werewolf," *Films and Filming*, VI (September, 1960), 15.

Connor, Edward, "The Return of the Dead," *Films in Review*, XV (March, 1964), 146-160.

Cutts, John, "*Vampyr*," *Films and Filming*, VII (December, 1960), 17-19.

Delahaye, Michel, "Between Heaven and Hell: Interview with Carl Dreyer," *Cahiers du Cinema in English*, No. 4 (1966), 7-17.

Denne, John D., "Society and the Monster," *December*, No. 10, 180-183.

Descher, Donald, "Karl Freund," *Cinema* (California), V, No. 4, 24-26.

Dillard, R.H.W., "Even a Man Who Is Pure at Heart: Poetry and Danger in the Horror Film" in *Man and the Movies*, ed. by W.R. Robinson (Baton Rouge: Louisiana State University Press, 1967), 60-96.

————, "Horror Film as Metaphysical Fable: An Interview With R.H.W. Dillard," ed. by George Garrett, *Contempora*, II, No. 3 (1972), 43-47.

Dreyer, Carl, "Dreyer in Double Reflection: An Annotated Translation of Carl Dreyer's 1946 Essay, 'A Little on Film Style,' " ed. by Donald Skoller, *Cinema* (California), VI, No. 2, 8-15.

Durgnat, Raymond, "From Pleasure Palace to Libido Motel," *Films and Filming*, VIII (January, 1962), 15, 41, 46.

————, "Scream Louder, Live Longer: An Introduction to Screen Violence," *The Listener*, LXXII (December 3, 1964), 880-882.

————, "The 'Yellow Peril' Rides Again," *Film Society Review*, V (October, 1969), 36-41.

Dyer, Peter John, "Z Films," *Sight and Sound*, XXXIII (Autumn, 1964), 179-181.

Ebert, R., "Just Another Horror Movie or Is It?," *Reader's Digest*, XCIV (June, 1969), 127-128.

Edwards, Roy, "Movie Gothick," *Sight and Sound*, XXVII (Autumn, 1957), 95-98.

Ehrenstein, David, "Black Sundae," *December*, XII (1970), 155-157.

Ellison, Harlan, "Three Faces of Fear: A Theory of Film Horror from the Works of Val Lewton," *Cinema* (California), III (March, 1966), 4-8, 13-14.

Everson, William K., "A Family Tree of Monsters," *Film Culture*, I (January-March, 1954), 24-30.

————, "Horror Films," *Films in Review*, V (January, 1954), 12-23.

Farber, Stephen, "The New American Gothic," *Film Quarterly*, XX (Fall, 1966), 22-27.

————, "*Performance*: The Nightmare Journey," *Cinema* (California), VI, No. 2, 16-21.

Fellini, Federico, "Fellini on Fellini on *Satyricon*," *Cinema* (California), V, No. 3, 2-13.

————, "Satyricon," *Playboy*, XVII (May, 1970), 105-111, 120.

Fisher, Jack, "Three Paintings of Sex: The Films of Ken Russell," *The Film Journal*, II (September, 1972), 33-43.

Fisher, Terence, "Horror Is My Business," *Films and Filming*, X (July, 1964), 7-8.

Fuller, Richard, "First Love: A Personal Comment on Horror Movies," *The Film Journal*, II (January-March, 1973), 66-68.

Gehman, Richard, "The Hollywood Horrors," *Cosmopolitan*, CXLV (November, 1958), 38-42.

Geltzer, George, "Tod Browning," *Films in Review*, IV (October, 1953), 410-416.

Glazebrook, Philip, "The Anti-Heroes of Horror," *Films and Filming*, XIII (October, 1966), 36-37.

Gerard, Lillian, "Boris Karloff: The Man Behind the Myth," *Film Comment*, VI (Spring, 1970), 46-51.

Gordon, Alex, "Boris Karloff," *Cinema* (California), V, No. 1, 2-9.

Grotjahn, Martin, "Horror — Yes, It Can Do You Good," *Films and Filming*, V (November, 1958), 9.

Guillermo, Gilberto Perez, "Shadow and Substance," *Sight and Sound*, XXXVI (Summer, 1967), 150-153.

Guy, Rory, "Horror: The Browning Version," *Cinema* (California), I (June-July, 1963), 26-28.

Halliwell, Leslie, "The Baron, the Count, and Their Ghoul Friends," *Films and Filming*, XV (June, 1969), 12-16; (July, 1969), 13-16.

Hamblin, Dora Jane, "Go On, Frighten Us to Death, We Love It!," *Life*, LV (August 30, 1963), 40.

Hanson, Curtis Lee, "*The Mummy*," *Cinema* (California), II (March-April, 1965), 30-31.

Harrington, Curtis, "Ghoulies and Ghosties," *Sight and Sound*, XXI (April-June, 1952), 157-161.

Henderson, Brian, "Targets," *Film Heritage*, IV (Summer, 1969), 1-8.

Hill, Derek, "The Face of Horror," *Sight and Sound*, XXVIII (Winter, 1958-1959), 6-11.

Hoda, F., "Epouvante et Science-Fiction," *Positif* (November-December, 1954), 1-17.

Hoveyda, Fereydoun, "Les Grimaces du Demon," *Cahiers du Cinema*, XX (May, 1961), 48-57.

Hubler, R.G., "Scare 'Em to Death and Cash In: What Makes the Movie Horror-Thriller Scary and Why," *Saturday Evening Post*, CCXIV (May 23, 1942), 20-21.

Hughes, Eileen, "Old Rome a la Fellini," *Life*, LXVII (August 15, 1969), 56-59.

Kaminsky, Stuart M., "*Night of the Living Dead*: An Appreciation," *Cinefantastique*, IV, No. 1 (1975), 20, 23.

Kane, Joe, "Nuclear Films," *Take One*, II, 9-10.

Karloff, Boris, "My Life as a Monster," *Films and Filming*, IV (November, 1957), 11.

Kelman, Ken, "Dreyer," *Film Culture*, No. 35 (1964-65), 1-9.

Kinder, Marsha, and Beverle Houston, "Seeing Is Believing: *The Exorcist* and *Don't Look Now*," *Cinema* (California), No. 34 (1974), 22-23.

Knight, Arthur, "Tired Blood," *Saturday Review*, XLI (October 18, 1958), 57-58.

Kobler, J., "Master of Movie Horror," *Saturday Evening Post*, CCXXXII (March 19, 1960), 30-31.

Koszarski, Richard, "*Mad Love*," *Film Heritage*, V (Winter, 1969-70), 24-29.

Kracauer, Siegfried, "Hollywood's Terror Films: Do They Reflect an American State of Mind?," *Commentary*, II (August, 1946), 132-136.

Langman, Betsy, "Working With Fellini," *Mademoiselle*, LXX (January, 1970), 74-75.

Lewis, Joseph, "A Bloody Laugh," *The Point*, February 26, 1970, 14.

Losano, Wayne A., "The Vampire Rises Again in Films of the Seventies," *The Film Journal*, II (January-March, 1973), 60-62.

Lourie, Gene, "A Background to Horror," *Films and Filming*, VI (February, 1960), 14.

MacLochlainn, Alf, "Pointed Horror: The Films of Luis Buñuel and Georges Franju," *The Film Journal*, I (Summer, 1971), 16-21.

McConnell, Frank, "Rough Beast Slouching," *Kenyon Review*, No. 1 (1970), 109-120.

McConnell, James, "Fellini-Satyricon," *Psychology Today*, IV (December, 1970), 16.

McCullough, Paul, "A Pittsburgh Horror Story," *Take One*, IV, No. 6 (1974), 8-10.

McGuinness, Richard, "Film: The Night of the Living Dead," *The Village Voice*, December 25, 1969, p, 54.

Myers, Henry, "Weird and Wonderful," *Screen Writer*, I (July, 1945), 19-23.

Myhers, John, "Fellini's Continuing Autobiography," *Cinema* (California), VI, No. 2, 40-41.

Nichols, Bill, *"Walkabout,"* *Cinema* (California), VII, No. 1, 8-12.

Nolan, Jack Edmund, "Robert Siodmak," *Films in Review*, XX (April, 1969), 218-252.

O'Mealy, Joseph, *"Fellini Satyricon*: A Structural Analysis," *Film Heritage*, VI (Summer, 1971), 25-29.

Othman, F.C., "Gooseflesh Maestro," *Saturday Evening Post*, CCXV (March 27, 1943), 20-21.

Oudart, Jean-Pierre, "Humain, Trop Humain," *Cahiers du Cinema* (March, 1969), 57-58.

Pechter, William S., "The Director Vanishes," *Moviegoer* (Summer-Autumn, 1964), 37-50.

Perez, Michel, "Le Desespoir Puritan," *Positif* (February, 1968), 61-63.

———, "Le Cinéma Retrouvé: *Dr. Jekyll and Mr. Hyde,"* *Positif* (June, 1966), 130-134.

Pirie, David, "New Blood," *Sight and Sound* (Spring, 1971), pp. 73-75.

Polanski, Roman, "Satisfaction — A Most Pleasant Feeling," *Films and Filming*, XV (April, 1969), 15-18.

Price, James, "Hail Horrors, Hail Infernal World," *London Magazine*, new series II (February, 1963), 67-72.

Price, Vincent, "Black Cats and Cobwebs," *Films and Filming*, XV (August, 1969), 52-54.

Purdy, Strother, "Existential Surrealism: The Neglected Example of Buñuel's *The Exterminating Angel,"* *Film Heritage*, III (Summer, 1968), 28-34.

Reismer, Joel, and Bruce Kane, "An Interview With Roman Polanski," *Cinema* (California), V, No. 2, 11-15.

Ringel, Harry, "A Hank of Hair and a Piece of Bone," *The Film Journal*, II ,No. 4 (1975), 14-19.

Rosen, Robert, "Enslaved by the Queen of the Night: The Relationship of E.T.A. Hoffman," *Film Comment*, VI (Spring, 1970), 26-31.

Ross, T.J., "Roman Polanski, *Repulsion,* and the New Mythology," *Film Heritage*, IV (Winter, 1968-1969), 1-10.

Russell, Ken, "Ideas for Films," *Film* (January-February, 1959), 13-15.

_____, "Shock Treatment," *Films and Filming,* XVI (July, 1970), 8-12.

Schöler, Franz, "Die Erben des Marquis de Sade," *Film,* V (August, 1967), 10-17; (September, 1967), 10-18; (October, 1967), 12-19.

_____, ed., "Horror-Bilderbuch und Materialien zu den literaischer Dorläufern des Horror-Films," *Film,* V (November, 1967), 41-51.

Schrader, Paul, *"Sisters,"* Cinema, VIII (Spring, 1973), 38-39.

Siodmak, Curt, "In Defense of the Ghouls," *Screen Writer,* I (February, 1946), 1-6.

Stanbury, C.M., "Monsters in the Movies," *December,* X, No. 1 (1968), 174-177.

Stein, Elliott, "The Night of the Living Dead," *Sight and Sound* (Spring, 1970), 105.

Surmacz, Gary Anthony, "Anatomy of a Horror Film," *Cinefantastique,* IV, No. 1 (1975), 15-19, 21-22, 24-27.

Tarratt, Margaret, "Monsters From the Id," *Films and Filming,* XVII (December, 1970), 38-42; (January, 1971).

Taylor, Russell, "Encounter With Siodmak," *Sight and Sound,* XXVIII (Summer-Autumn, 1959), 180-182.

Thomaier, William, and Robert F. Fink, "James Whale," *Films in Review,* XIII (May, 1962), 277-296.

Thomas, John, "Freaks," *Film Quarterly,* XVII (Spring, 1964), 59-61.

Thomas, Kevin, "Roger Corman: The Director Who Changed the Face of Hollywood," *Los Angeles Times Calendar,* January 9, 1972.

Torok, Jean-Paul, "H Pictures," *Positif* (May, 1961), pp. 54-58; (July, 1961), 41-49.

Tourneur, Jacques, "Taste Without Cliches," *Films and Filming* (November, 1956), 9-11.

Tunley, R., "TV's Midnight Madness," *Saturday Evening Post,* CCXXXI (August 16, 1958), 19-21.

Vaughn, S., "Monster Movies?" *Library Journal,* XCVI (October 15, 1971), 3439-3441.

Weinberg, Herman and Gretchen, "*Vampyr* — An Interview With Baron de Gunzberg," *Film Culture* (Spring, 1964), 57-59.

Wood, Robin, "In Memorium Michael Reeves," *Movie* (Winter, 1969-1970), 2-6.

PERIODICALS

There have been a number of magazines devoted to the horror film (and fantasy and science fiction films), most of them fan magazines devoted to the pun as much as to the films themselves. Forrest J. Ackerman's *Famous Monsters of Filmland* and its stablemate for a time, *Monster World,* deserve mention for their pioneering efforts in the field and their ability to make available a wealth of useful information squeezed in between the bad jokes and ads for face fur and monster feet. The detailed and roughly accurate summaries of films which appear in *Famous Monsters* from time to time are particularly helpful. Calvin Thomas Beck's *Castle of Frankenstein* has always been plagued by distribution problems, but it is a serious cut above Ackerman's magazines in quality and serious intent. It and the relatively new *Cinefantastique,* which carries that seriousness and quality even further, are certainly the best magazines having to do with horror films published in this country today. The French magazines, *Bizarre* and the totally serious *Midi-Minuit Fantastique,* are the only other magazines successfully devoted to the genre. A glance at the list of articles in this bibliography will show which other film magazines are most open to the horror film as a subject for enquiry and analysis.